Contents

Special Holiday Messages

by Susan L. Lingo

Standard
PUBLISHING
CINCINNATI, OHIO

Dedication

Acknowledge and take to heart this day that the Lord is God in heaven above and on the earth below. There is no other.

Deuteronomy 4:39

Bible Message Make-n-Takes
©1998 Susan L. Lingo

Published by The Standard Publishing Company, Cincinnati, Ohio 45231. A division of Standex International Corporation.

Credits
Produced by Susan L. Lingo, Bright Ideas Books
Cover design and Illustration by Liz Howe
Illustrated by Marilynn G. Barr

06 05 04 03 02   8 7 6 5 4

0-7847-0838-X ISBN
Printed in the United States of America

Introduction

What do children's leaders gobble up faster than chocolate cake at a picnic? Quick devotions! Think about it. Between Sunday school, Vacation Bible School, children's church, and sermon time, you probably go through about two hundred quick devotions and mini-messages a year. But how many messages do your children really remember? Which devotions do kids actually apply in their lives? In other words, *what do your kids take away from the message time?* Just words—until now! *Bible Message Make-n-Takes* is a first-of-its-kind devotion book with memorable messages kids truly "take away." Cool craft projects that apply to devotional messages are paired with clever "Take-It-Away" cards that sum up the message and the accompanying Scripture verse. (Collect the cards on a clip or key chain and use them for quick reviews and instant games!)

Powerful, God-centered messages, cool crafts, collectible cards...what could be better? **Flexibility for you!** The "Choose-n-Use Options" included with each message allow you to lengthen the learning for up to an hour—or use the activities later as lively message reviews.

Use *Bible Message Make-n-Takes* to enliven children's message time in adult church, to enrich Sunday school or VBS lessons, or to perk up children's church themes. Whenever you reach for *Bible Message Make-n-Takes,* you'll be providing your kids powerful Bible truths with the make it-take it appeal of quick crafts. So what are you waiting for? TAKE IT AWAY!

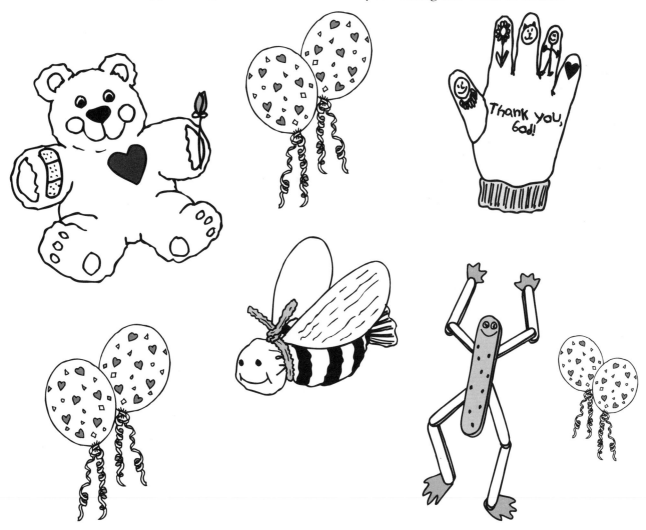

1. Prayer Bears

Decorate darling stuffed bears and learn the importance of praying for others.

Point to Make: Jesus wants us to pray for others.

Verse to View: I pray for them. *John 17:9*

Preparation: You'll need a Bible, red felt, scissors, small plastic bandages, small silk flowers, Tacky craft glue, and a photocopy of Take-It-Away Card 1 for each child. You'll also need a 4-inch-tall stuffed bear for each child.

Purchase inexpensive 4-inch-tall stuffed bears from a craft store. Cut a 1/2-inch felt heart for each child.

The Message

Gather children and hold up a stuffed bear. Ask:
- **How can a teddy bear help someone feel loved?**
- **What other actions help us feel loved? How can we show our love?**
- **In what ways does praying for others show our love?**

Say: **Jesus knew how important it was to show love by praying for his friends and other people. In fact, Jesus prayed for his friends the night before he died. Jesus talked to God and said, "I pray for them... for they are yours." How did Jesus' prayers for others show his love?** Allow children to tell their ideas, then read aloud John 17:9 from the Bible. Say: **Jesus prayed for others, and we can pray for others too. We can make Prayer Bears to remind us to pray for other people.**

The Meaning

Hand each child a stuffed bear, a felt heart, a small silk flower, and a small bandage. Have children glue the felt hearts on their bears as you say: **Hearts remind us of love. We can use our hearts to pray for other people's feelings and happiness. And we can ask God**

to spread love to their hearts and lives. Have children glue small silk flowers on the bears' paws while you say: **The flowers remind us to ask God for ways we can be kind to others.** Stick the small bandages on the bears' legs or foreheads as you say: **Bandages remind us of hurts and illnesses. We can pray for people who are sick or hurt or have other needs God can meet. When we pray for the needs of others, God listens! That's why it's important to pray for others.**

Now hold your Prayer Bears and silently think of one person you can pray for this week. (Pause.) Say: **Let's pray. Dear God, we're glad Jesus loved us and prayed for us. Please help us show our love by praying for others as Jesus did. Amen.**

Let's close with a special Take-It-Away Card you can take home along with your Prayer Bear.

Take-It-Away Card

Hand Take-It-Away Card 1 to each child as you close the message time. Have one volunteer read aloud the "Point to Make" and another the "Verse to View." End by challenging children to read the card often.

Choose-n-Use Options

> Message 1—Prayer Bears
> Jesus wants us to pray for others.
>
> **I pray for them.**
> John 17:9

- Make a colorful prayer chain to hang in your classroom. Cut 6-by-2-inch strips of construction paper. Have children write on the strips the names of people your class could pray for, such as the minister, government leaders, missionaries your church supports, children in hospitals, or people in war-torn countries. Assemble the strips into a prayer "chain." Pray for a different "link" in your chain of love each time you gather.

- Read aloud Luke 11:1-4 and visit about why Jesus taught his disciples to pray. Ask questions such as "Why do you think the disciples wanted Jesus to teach them to pray?" and "What kinds of things do you think the disciples prayed for?" Teach your children the Lord's Prayer and point out that Jesus used the words "us" and "our" several times to encourage us to pray for all of us to avoid temptation, for God to forgive our sins, and to thank God for our daily food.

2. The Inside Story.

Surprise crayon etchings reveal it's "what's inside" that counts.

Point to Make: God looks at our hearts—not our outward appearances.

Verse to View: The Lord looks at the heart.   1 Samuel 16:7

Preparation: You'll need a Bible, white legal-size envelopes, crayons, scissors, poster board, pennies, and a photocopy of Take-It-Away Card 2 for each child.

Before the message time, cut a 1-inch poster-board heart and flower shape for each child. Prepare an envelope for each child by placing a heart, flower, and penny in an envelope and sealing it shut.

The Message

Gather children and hold up an envelope. Ask children to describe what they see. Answers might include "a white envelope," "a long envelope," and "a thin envelope to mail letters." Then say: **The way we see this envelope is a lot like the way we see people. We see what they look like on the outside. But God sees us a different way. Let's read from the Bible about how God sees us. When you know what God sees, put your hands on your hearts.** Read aloud 1 Samuel 16:7, then ask:

● **What does God look at?**
● **Why do you think God looks at our hearts and not our outward appearances?**

Say: **God knows the true person is on the inside. The condition of our hearts tells so much—whether we're kind to others, if our faith is real, and if we truly love God.** Hold up an envelope again and say: **Looking at the outside of this envelope doesn't tell much, just like looking at the outsides of people. So let's take a surprise "peek" at some envelopes to see what's inside.**

The Meaning

Hand each child a crayon and an envelope containing the "surprise" objects. As you talk, have children place the envelopes on the floor and gently rub back and forth across them with the crayons. Say: **Oh, my! What's on the insides of the envelopes?** Encourage children to identify the hearts, flowers, and pennies. Say: **The heart shape reminds us that when God sees our hearts, he knows all the feelings and thoughts inside us. The flower shape is for the way God knows the kind ways we treat and think about others. And the penny represents the way God sees our worries. Some people worry about money or school or other things, but God knows each of our worries—even before we do!** Ask:

● **How would it help us to look at people's hearts and not their outward appearances?**

● **Who can you take a kinder, closer look at this week?**

Say: **Let's share a prayer about not judging others by the way they look on the outside but rather seeing the good things in their hearts. Dear God, thank you for loving us enough to look past our outside appearances. Help us be more understanding of others as we look at their hearts. In Jesus' name, amen.**

Let's close with a special Take-It-Away Card you can take home along with your surprise envelope.

Take-It-Away Card

Hand Take-It-Away Card 2 to each child as you close the message time. Have one volunteer read aloud the "Point to Make" and another the "Verse to View." End by challenging children to read the card often.

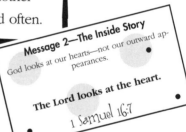

Message 2—The Inside Story

God looks at our hearts—not our outward appearances.

The Lord looks at the heart.

1 Samuel 16:7

Choose-n-Use Options

● Provide fruits such as bananas, apples, and oranges. Form pairs and decide which partner will be the Outside Artist and which will be the Inside Artist. Have Outside Artists draw the outsides of the fruits and Inside Artists draw what they think is on the inside. Then cut open the fruits and compare illustrations. Point out how we may think we know what's on the inside but, on closer inspection, find we've missed important features. End by sharing the delicious fruit and thanking God for his perfect view of our hearts.

● Brainstorm the good traits inside the hearts of biblical characters such as Noah, Joshua, David, Abigail, and Jesus. Include traits such as kindness, faithfulness, a love for God, and honesty. Visit about why each of these traits is more important than the outward appearances of these people. Ask children how they can nurture the same traits inside their own hearts.

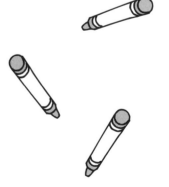

3. Love That Light!

Clever candles will de-LIGHT children as they shine their love to others.

Point to Make: We can shine our love to others.

Verse to View: You are the light of the world. Matthew 5:14

Preparation: You'll need a Bible, ribbon, scissors, sticky tack, chunky 2-inch candles, a variety of dried beans, clean baby food jars with lids, matches, and a photocopy of Take-It-Away Card 3 for each child.

Before the message time, cut a 6-inch piece of ribbon for each child. Be sure you have a chunky candle and baby food jar with lid for each child and enough dried beans to fill the jars halfway. Purchase sticky tack at discount stores or office supply centers.

The Message

Gather children and hold up a candle. Ask children what candles are used for. Then light the candle and say: **If we were in a dark room and had this candle, it would shine its light for all of us to enjoy and use. A candle's light doesn't shine for just one person—its light spreads to others. Did you know Jesus said we're like bright lights who can shine our love to others? Let's read what Jesus said.** Blow out the candle, then read aloud Matthew 5:14-16 from the Bible. Ask:

▲ **What did Jesus mean when he said we're like lights that shouldn't be hidden?**

▲ **How is our love like a bright light?**

▲ **What happens when we hide our love from other people?**

Say: **When we shine the light of our love to others, we're also shining the love of Jesus on them! Isn't that wonderful? Let's make beautiful candle-jar lights to remind us how important it is to shine our love to others.**

The Meaning

Hand each child a baby food jar, piece of ribbon, glob of sticky tack, and a small candle. Help children fill their jars halfway with dried beans. Point out how the beans represent all the people we can shine our love to. Have children tie ribbon bows around the necks of the jars, then use sticky tack to attach the candles to the jar lids. As you work, ask:

▲ **How can we spread our light and shine our love to others?**

▲ **Who can you shine on this week?**

Say: **Tonight, place your candle-jar on the dinner table and ask an adult to light the candle. Then turn off the lights and say a prayer asking God to help each of you to shine your love—and Jesus' love—to others all week long.**

Let's close with a special Take-It-Away Card you can take home along with your lovely candle-jar light.

Take-It-Away Card

Hand Take-It-Away Card 3 to each child as you close the message time. Have one volunteer read aloud the "Point to Make" and another the "Verse to View." End by challenging children to read the card often.

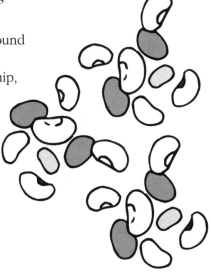

Message 3—Love That Light!
We can shine our love to others.

You are the light of the world.
Matthew 5:14

Choose-n-Use Options

▲ Use unlit candle-jar lights while you sing lively songs. Lead children in singing "This Little Light of Mine" and holding the candle-jars high, waving them gently back and forth or tapping them gently on their knees. When you sing the words "let it shine, let it shine, let it shine," have children hold their candle-jars above the heads of other children. End by singing "Shine, Jesus, Shine."

▲ Use a lit candle to create a quiet atmosphere of worship. Gather around the candle and explain that worship is a way we spread our "love-lights" to God. Visit about ways to shine love to God through worship, reading the Bible, praying, being kind to others, and telling others about Jesus. Then join hands and have each child quietly pray by completing the following sentence: "I will shine my love to you, God, by . . ." End with "amen," then let children gently blow out the candle.

4. Wave Your Choice

Colorful bicycle flags will have kids showing off their
"Number One Choice!"

Point to Make: We choose to serve God.

Verse to View: But as for me and my household,
we will serve the Lord.   *Joshua 24:15*

Preparation: You'll need a Bible, a yard of white vinyl, permanent markers, scissors, several yards of 19-gauge steel wire, clear packing tape, and a photocopy of Take-It-Away Card 4 for each child.

Cut a 2-foot piece of steel wire for each child. Cut the white vinyl into 8-by-12-inch rectangles. Cut one rectangle for each child.

The Message

Set out the craft materials and invite each child to choose one item to hold. Then ask:
■ **Why did you choose that particular item?**
■ **What does "making a choice" mean?**
■ **Why is it important to make good choices?**
Say: **Choosing means deciding. It means picking something above everything else, just as you chose your craft item over the other items. Making good choices is very important. Did you know that each day we make the choice to serve God? And because God is the most important part of our lives, choosing to serve God is the most important choice we'll ever make! Let's read what the Bible says about choosing to serve God.** Read aloud Joshua 24:15, then ask:
■ **Why is choosing to serve God a good choice?**
■ **How does choosing to serve God show him our love? show others we love God?**
Say: **We can show others we choose to serve God by making neat flags to wave from our bicycles!**

The Meaning

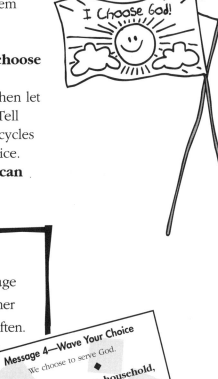

Be sure each child has a vinyl rectangle and piece of wire. Help children write the words "I Choose God!" on the vinyl. Then let them decorate the flags any way they choose. As children work, ask:

■ **What are ways we can serve God?**

■ **How can we help others realize how important it is to choose God?**

When the flags are done, tape them to the tops of the wires. Then let children hold their flags high and say, "We choose to serve God!" Tell children to ask an adult to attach the wires to the backs of their bicycles so everyone can see their colorful "high-flying" declarations of choice.

Then say: **Let's close with a special Take-It-Away Card you can take home along with your bike flag.**

Take-It-Away Card

Hand Take-It-Away Card 4 to each child as you close the message time. Have one volunteer read aloud the "Point to Make" and another the "Verse to View." End by challenging children to read the card often.

Message 4—Wave Your Choice

We choose to serve God.

But as for me and my household, we will serve the Lord.

Joshua 24:15

Choose-n-Use Options

■ Set out pretzel sticks and chunks of fresh fruits and cheeses. Invite children to make "snack-kabobs" by choosing which fruits and cheeses to add and in what order to skewer them on pretzel sticks. Point out that making food choices is fun but not as important as choosing to serve God. As you nibble your goodies, visit about the good things that come from choosing God and what might happen if we don't make this good choice.

■ Form pairs and invite partners to look through the book of Psalms to choose a phrase or short psalm to read aloud to the class. When all the verses are read, point out that choosing to read God's Word is a good choice. Explain that one way we show we've chosen to serve God is through reading the Bible and learning more about God and his Word.

5. Temper Tornadoes

Raging "storms" in a jar help kids understand anger control.

Point to Make: Prayer calms our anger.

Verse to View: Get rid of all bitterness, rage and anger.
Ephesians 4:31

Preparation: You'll need a Bible, water, liquid dish soap, green food coloring, and a photocopy of Take-It-Away Card 5 for each child. You'll also need a clear plastic soda bottle and top for each child.

Fill the clear plastic bottles 3/4 full of water. Prepare a "Temper Tornado" bottle by following the directions in this activity. Practice making "tornadoes" by setting the bottle on a table and rapidly swirling the bottle in a circular motion.

The Message

Gather children and ask:
- **What things make you really angry?**
- **How do you act when you're very upset?**
- **In what ways can anger hurt you? hurt others? hurt God?**

Rapidly swirl the "Temper Tornado" bottle and say: **Anger is a lot like a nasty storm. Just as storms build and become more fierce, anger can build and grow more fierce. We may angrily thunder bad words at others or strike at them like lightning bolts. And when we don't control our anger, it rains on everyone around us. Ugh—what an "angry storm!"** Stop swirling the bottle and watch the "storm." **Let's see what God says about anger.** Read aloud Ephesians 4:31, 32, then ask:
- **What does God tell us to do with anger?**
- **How do we treat others when we control our anger?**
- **What are good ways to control our anger?**

Encourage children to name ways such as talking about our feelings, drawing pictures of what makes us angry, asking God to take away our anger, or redirecting negative feelings through kind deeds.

Say: **Prayer is another good way to control anger. Talking to God and telling him our feelings helps. And so does asking God to help us be forgiving instead of angry. Let's make Temper Tornadoes as reminders of how prayer helps us calm anger.**

The Meaning

Hand each child a plastic bottle with water. Have children remove the bottle tops and add several drops of liquid soap and food coloring. Securely replace the bottle tops, then have children swirl the bottles on the floor in an upright position. As the storms form, say: **When we feel angry storms building inside, it's time to pray and ask God's help in calming those storms. So let's stop swirling our bottles and pray.** (Pause.) **Dear God, help us turn to you when we're angry. Teach us to have forgiveness instead of anger. Thank you for calming our angry feelings and putting sunshine back in our hearts. In Jesus' name, amen.**

Look at your bottles. See how the storms are calm now? In the time it takes to pray, our anger calms. Isn't that great? Now let's close with a special Take-It-Away Card you can take home along with your Temper Tornado.

Take-It-Away Card

Hand Take-It-Away Card 5 to each child as you close the message time. Have one volunteer read aloud the "Point to Make" and another the "Verse to View." End by challenging children to read the card often.

Choose-n-Use Options

Message 5—Temper Tornadoes
Prayer calms our anger.

Get rid of all bitterness, rage and anger.
Ephesians 4:31

- Cut out a large paper heart. Have children sit in a circle and pass the paper heart. As children hold the heart, have them each name one thing that makes them angry and then tear away a piece of the heart. Point out that anger hurts people's feelings and makes them feel "torn up" and unhappy inside. Talk about ways to handle anger so it doesn't hurt others. Include ways such as praying, showing patience and love, counting to ten, or "talking it out." Let children tear out paper hearts and decorate them as reminders to show love instead of anger.

- Form small groups and assign each group one of the following verses to quietly read: Proverbs 15:18; Colossians 3:8; Proverbs 29:22; and Ephesians 4:32. Invite groups to brainstorm ways of pantomiming the verses and then to act out the verses. See if the other children can guess the meaning of each verse, then have groups read aloud their verses. End with a prayer thanking God for helping us deal with anger through prayer, kindness, patience, and forgiveness.

6. Hip-Hop!

Funny frogs help kids remember that our word is important to God.

Point to Make: When we tell God we'll do something, we hop to it!

Verse to View: Jonah obeyed the word of the Lord
and went to Nineveh. *Jonah 3:3*

Preparation: You'll need a Bible, green markers or crayons, craft sticks, tongue depressors, Tacky craft glue, small wiggly craft eyes, green construction paper, three copies of the frog illustration, and a photocopy of Take-It-Away Card 6 for each child.

Enlarge and make three green photocopies of the frog on the lily pad. Be sure you have one tongue depressor, eight craft sticks, and one pair of wiggly eyes for each child.

The Message

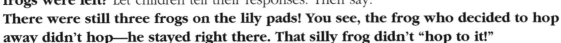

Hold up the three green paper frogs. Say: **Once there were three green frogs sitting on lily pads. One day, one of the frogs decided to hop away. How many frogs were left?** Let children tell their responses. Then say: **There were still three frogs on the lily pads! You see, the frog who decided to hop away didn't hop—he stayed right there. That silly frog didn't "hop to it!"**

▲ **In what ways are we like the frog when we say we'll do something but don't do it?**

▲ **How do you think God feels when we say we'll do something for him but we don't "hop to it"?**

▲ **Why is it important to do what we say we'll do?**

Say: **When we do what we say we're going to do, that's called "keeping our word." That's how we show others we can be trusted. Did you know that God trusts us to keep our word? In other words, God trusts us to "hop to it" when we say we'll do something for him. What are things we often tell God we'll do?** Allow children to share their ideas and encourage them to name things such as reading the Bible, being nice to brothers or sisters, or praying each day. Then ask:

▲ **Why is it important to keep our word to God?**

Say: **Let's make fun frogs to remind us to "hop to it" for God!**

The Meaning

Hand each child a tongue depressor, eight craft sticks, and a pair of wiggly eyes. Have children use green markers or crayons to color the craft sticks and tongue depressors. Show children how to glue two craft sticks together to make a bent frog "leg." Then glue the legs to the sides of the tongue depressors. Tear "froggy legs" from green paper and glue them to the ends of the craft sticks. Finally, glue wiggly eyes to the "froggy heads."

As you work, say: **Let's see what the Bible says about keeping our word and doing what we say we will.** Read aloud Jonah 3:3. Then say: **Our word is important to God. So when we tell God we'll do something, we want to hop to it! God wants us to have faith in action—not just words.**

Let's close with a special Take-It-Away Card you can take home along with your hoppity frog.

Take-It-Away Card

Hand Take-It-Away Card 6 to each child as you close the message time. Have one volunteer read aloud the "Point to Make" and another the "Verse to View." End by challenging children to read the card often.

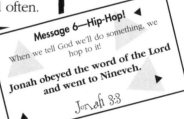

Message 6—Hip-Hop!
When we tell God we'll do something, we hop to it!

Jonah obeyed the word of the Lord and went to Nineveh.

Jonah 3:3

Choose-n-Use Options

▲ Have a lively leapfrog relay. Form pairs and have partners place their frogs at one end of the playing area. Line partners up at the opposite end and let them leapfrog to retrieve their wooden frogs, then return to the starting places. Switch partners and play again.

▲ Invite children to use their Bibles to read aloud the stories of three Bible characters who "hopped to it" for God. Read about Jonah's decision to go to Nineveh (Jonah 3:1-3), Joshua at the walls of Jericho (Joshua 6:1-7), and Joseph when he took Mary and baby Jesus to Egypt (Matthew 2:13, 14). Visit about what might have happened if these people had not "hopped to it" when God called them to obey.

7. Mezuzah Tubes

Wood-grained tubes remind kids of the importance of God's Word.

Point to Make: God's Word is important to learn and remember.

Verse to View: I will not neglect your word.   Psalm 119:16

Preparation: You'll need a Bible, cardboard tubes, wood-grained Con-Tact paper, brown yarn, aluminum foil, scissors, clear tape, and a bag of small rubber bands. You'll also need photocopies of the Scripture verses on page 106 and a photocopy of Take-It-Away Card 7 for each child.

Cut an 8-inch length of brown yarn and a 4 1/4-by-6-inch piece of wood-grained Con-Tact paper for each child. Prepare a "Mezuzah Tube" with a Scripture inside according to the directions on page 19.

The Message

Hold up the Mezuzah Tube you made before class. Shake the tube and ask children to guess what's inside. Then have a child pull out a Scripture scroll and read the verse aloud. Ask:

■ **Where are these words from?**
■ **Why do you think God's Word is important?**
■ **How does knowing God's Word help us every day?**
■ **Why does God want us to learn his Word?**

Say: **God's Word is very important because it teaches us how to live the way God commands us. God's Word protects us, helps us in times of trouble, and is always true. In Bible times, God told the people to keep his Word close to them all the time. Let's see what the Bible says about the importance of learning God's Word and keeping it close to us.**

Read aloud Psalm 119:16. **God commanded the people of the Old Testament to write his Word on their doorposts and keep it close. The people obeyed and made little boxes or tubes called "Mezuzahs." They wrote down God's Word and kept it in the Mezuzahs beside their doors. Let's make Mezuzah Tubes to remind us that God's Word is important to learn and remember.**

The Meaning

Hand each child a cardboard tube, small piece of aluminum foil, piece of Con-Tact paper, and length of yarn. Have children wrap the foil securely over one end of their tubes. Then help children wrap the sides of their tubes with wood-grained paper, being sure to catch the ends of the foil in the Con-Tact paper. Tape brown yarn to the open tops of the tubes as loop "handles." As you work, ask questions such as "How can we learn God's Word?" "When does God's Word help us?" and "Why is it important to keep God's Word close to us all the time?"

When the Mezuzah Tubes are complete, hand each child a photocopy of the Scripture verses to cut apart. Roll the verses in scrolls and slide rubber bands around them. Read aloud the verses as you roll the scrolls. Have children tuck the Scripture scrolls inside their Mezuzah Tubes. Encourage children to hang the tubes in their homes and read the verses to their families often.

Then say: **Let's close with a special Take-It-Away Card you can take home along with your Mezuzah Tube.**

Take-It-Away Card

Hand Take-It-Away Card 7 to each child as you close the message time. Have one volunteer read aloud the "Point to Make" and another the "Verse to View." End by challenging children to read the card often.

> **Message 7—Mezuzah Tubes**
> God's Word is important to learn and
> ◆ remember.
>
> ■ **I will not neglect your word.**
> Psalm 119:16 ■

Choose-n-Use Options

■ One of the best ways to learn God's Word is by singing it! Sing Ephesians 4:32 to the tune of "Ten Little Indians"—*"Be kind and loving to each other. Be kind and loving to each other. Be kind and loving to each other—Ephesians 4:32!"* (ICB) Shake each other's hands or give one another pats on the shoulder as you sing.

■ Challenge older children to read sections of Psalm 119 in pairs or trios and to list all the verses that mention God's Word, commands, laws, or decrees and statutes. Explain that God's decrees and statutes are his law and his Word. Read these verse sections: Psalm 119:9-16, 17-24, 33-40, 41-48, 49-56, 97-104, and 105-112.

8. Hide It in Your Heart

Wearable hearts with a hidden message teach about God's Word.

Point to Make: God's Word is alive in our hearts.

Verse to View: I have hidden your word in my heart.
Psalm 119:11

Preparation: You'll need a Bible, red felt, scissors, Tacky craft glue, photocopies of the Scripture heart below, a 6-inch strip of Velcro for each child (the rough portion), and a photocopy of Take-It-Away Card 8 for each child.

Photocopy and cut out one Scripture heart below for each child. Use the hearts as patterns to cut out red felt hearts. Prepare one paper Scripture heart and two felt hearts for each child.

The Message

Gather children and hold up a felt heart. Ask children what a heart symbolizes and what things they love in their hearts. Then say: **We all feel love in our hearts for many different things and people—and especially God. In the Bible, God told us something special to do with our hearts. I'll read from the Bible. When you know what God wants us to do with our hearts, cover your heart with your hand.** Read aloud Psalm 119:11. Then ask:

● **What are we to do with our hearts?**
● **Why are we to hide God's Word in our hearts?**

Say: **God wants us to use our hearts as hiding places for his Word. God wants his Word alive in our hearts so we'll know the good ways he wants us to live. When we hide God's Word in our hearts, we won't do or say things that God dislikes. It's important to remember to hide God's Word in our hearts, so let's make wearable hearts with God's hidden Word on them.**

I have hidden your word in my heart. Psalm 119:11

The Meaning

Hand each child two felt hearts, a paper Scripture heart, and a rough Velcro strip portion. Have children glue the paper Scripture hearts to one of the felt hearts. Then carefully glue the tops of the hearts to the second felt heart so the verse can be seen when the top heart is lifted. As you work, talk about ways to hide God's Word in your hearts, such as reading the Bible, memorizing Scripture, and obeying what God's Word tell us.

Have children wrap the Velcro strips around their wrists as "bracelets," then stick the felt hearts to the bracelets. Let children take turns lifting their hearts and reading God's Word. Say: **God wants us to hide his Word in our hearts so we can put his Word to use in our lives. God's Word teaches us, protects us, helps us in times of trouble—and brings us great joy! Wear your special hearts home and remember that God's Word is alive in our hearts!**

Let's close with a special Take-It-Away Card you can take home along with your Scripture-heart bracelet.

Take-It-Away Card

Hand Take-It-Away Card 8 to each child as you close the message time. Have one volunteer read aloud the "Point to Make" and another the "Verse to View." End by challenging children to read the card often.

Message 8—Hide It in Your Heart
God's Word is alive in our hearts.

I have hidden your word in my heart.

Psalm 119:11

Choose-n-Use Options

- Let children make "anytime valentines" to share God's Word with others. Provide construction paper, paper doilies, glue sticks, markers, scissors, and ribbon. Have children cut out paper hearts and decorate them with craft materials, then write Psalm 119:11, 16, or 105 on the backs of the hearts. Encourage children to give the lovely Scripture hearts to someone they love.

- Cut out paper hearts in various sizes and shapes. Choose one or two Scripture verses you'd like your children to learn and write one word from each verse on each heart. Hide the hearts around the room, then invite children to go on a Scripture scavenger hunt. Reassemble the verses when all the hearts are found, then discuss what each verse means.

9. Teacher, Teach Me

Cute chalkboards help kids understand the ABC's of being teachable.

Point to Make: God wants us to be teachable.

Verse to View: I am the Lord your God, who teaches you what is best for you. Isaiah 48:17

Preparation: You'll need a Bible, colored chalk, Tacky craft glue, legal-size envelopes, black craft felt, scissors, markers, and a photocopy of Take-It-Away Card 9 for each child. You'll also need a small craft chalkboard for each child.

Purchase felt and inexpensive chalkboard "slates" from a craft store. Cut the black felt into 4-inch squares, one for each child. Be sure you have one stick of chalk and one envelope for each child.

The Message

Gather children and hold up a small chalkboard. Ask children to identify the slate and what it's used for in school. Then ask:

▲ **What kinds of things do we learn in school? in our families? in church or Sunday school?**

▲ **What happens if we're not teachable and never learn about important things?**

▲ **Why is it important to be teachable when we're learning about God?**

Say: **Being teachable means we want to learn new things. When we're teachable, we learn right from wrong and good from bad—and we make good choices about how to live, what to say, and what to do. Why do you think God wants us to be teachable?**

Allow children time to share their ideas. Then say: **Let's learn what the Bible says about being teachable.**

Read aloud Isaiah 48:17, then say: **Being teachable means we don't act as though we "know it all." It's admitting we have a lot to learn—and we always have a lot to learn when it comes to knowing about God! Let's make a fun slate and learn a bit more about being teachable.**

The Meaning

Hand each child a chalkboard, an envelope, a stick of chalk, and a felt "eraser." Help children glue the envelopes to the backs of the chalkboards with the open sides showing. Explain that the envelopes are holders for their felt erasers and chalk. Use markers to draw designs on the wooden frames of the slates. Then have children use their chalk to write the letter A on the fronts of their slates. Say: **A is for the word "Always."** Have children write the letter B, then say: **B stands for the word "Be."** What letter comes next? When children say C, explain: **Today, a different letter comes next! Let's write a T because T stands for the word "Teachable"—and that's what we want to be! When we're teachable, we learn about God and then put that learning to work in our lives.**

Now let's close with a special Take-It-Away Card to take home along with your special chalkboard.

Take-It-Away Card

Hand Take-It-Away Card 9 to each child as you close the message time. Have one volunteer read aloud the "Point to Make" and another the "Verse to View." End by challenging children to read the card often.

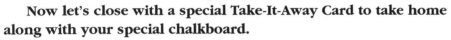

Message 9—Teacher, Teach Me
God wants us to be teachable.
I am the Lord your God, who teaches you what is best for you.
Isaiah 48:17

Choose-n-Use Options

▲ Use your chalkboards to play a fun word game—and to learn more about God. Think of a word that describes God, such as love, powerful, or faithful. Then draw on the chalkboard as many spaces as there are letters in the word. Let children guess letters to fill in the spaces. When the word is complete, have children each tell one way God has been loving, powerful, or faithful in their lives.

▲ Read aloud the story from Luke 2:41-52 of Jesus staying in the temple as a young boy. Discuss why Jesus wanted to listen to the teachers and ask questions. Ask questions such as "What was Jesus doing in the temple?" "How did Jesus show he was teachable?" and "Why is it good to share teaching about God with others?" Point out that Jesus continued to grow in wisdom (Luke 2:52) because he was teachable.

10. The Golden Ruler

Real rulers remind kids to treat others "immeasurably" good!

Point to Make: We treat others as we want to be treated.

Verse to View: Do to others what you would
have them do to you.   Matthew 7:12

Preparation: You'll need a Bible, several vinyl tape measures, scissors, thin gold braid, a paper punch, heart stickers, a yardstick, a ruler, and a photocopy of Take-It-Away Card 10 for each child.

Purchase yellow vinyl tape measures from a fabric store or discount center. Cut the measuring tapes into 8-inch segments and the gold braid into 6-inch pieces. Punch a hole at one end of each measuring tape segment. Be sure you have two matching heart stickers for each child.

The Message

Hold up the ruler, the yardstick, and a piece of tape measure. Ask:
- **How do these tools help us measure length?**
- **How do we measure the way we treat others?**

Say: **There is one tool that helps us know how to measure the way we treat others— and that tool is the Bible.** Hold up the Bible. **In the Bible, Jesus tells us the right way to treat people. Let's see what Jesus said.** Read aloud Matthew 7:12, then ask:
- **What did Jesus say about treating other people?**

Say: **Jesus said to treat others the way we want to be treated. This is what many people call the "Golden Rule," and it's a great way to measure how we're treating others. Let's make Golden Rulers to remind us of the Golden Rule.**

The Meaning

Hand each child a segment of measuring tape, a piece of gold braid, and two heart stickers. Help each child tie one end of his or her gold braid through the hole in the tape measure.

Then sandwich the other end of the gold braid between two heart stickers. As you work, ask children how they like to be treated. Then say: **We like to be treated with kindness, respect, helpfulness, forgiveness—in other words, we like to be treated with love! And that's what the Golden Rule is all about. Use your special Golden Ruler as a Bible bookmark. When you look at the lines on your ruler, think of all the people you can treat with love today and every day. Let's pray. Dear God, thank you for your love. Help us always to remember to treat others as we want to be treated. Amen.**

Let's close with a special Take-It-Away Card you can take home along with your Golden Ruler.

Take-It-Away Card

Hand Take-It-Away Card 10 to each child as you close the message time. Have one volunteer read aloud the "Point to Make" and another the "Verse to View." End by challenging children to read the card often.

Message 10—The Golden Ruler
We treat others as we want to be treated.

Do to others what you would have them do to you.

Matthew 7:12

Choose-n-Use Options

■ Stretch a retractable carpenter's measure down the center of your play area. Invite children to take turns seeing how far they can hop, step, and jump. Each time a child takes a turn, have him or her tell the first name of someone to treat with love, kindness, and respect.

■ List pairs of biblical characters who were friends. Use pairs such as David and Jonathan, Ruth and Naomi, and Moses and Joshua. Discuss how these friends treated each other. Then read aloud Matthew 5:43, 44 and talk about why Jesus wants us to treat even people who may not be close friends with kindness and love.

■ Hand each child two slips of paper and a pencil. Ask children to list two ways they'd like to be treated and write each way on a slip of paper. For example, children might wish to be treated with respect or to be treated fairly or in a less childlike manner. Collect all the papers, then take turns reading them aloud. See how many similar responses there are, then discuss why each response is important.

11. Kindness Confetti

Cute coin purses encourage children to speak positively.

Point to Make: God wants us to speak kindly.

Verse to View: Therefore encourage one another.

1 Thessalonians 5:11

Preparation: You'll need a Bible, black permanent markers, black confetti, multi-colored confetti, and a photocopy of Take-It-Away Card 11 for each child. You'll also need a pliable plastic coin purse for each child.

Purchase soft, "squeeze-open" coin purses from a discount store. Purchase ready-made confetti or punch out your own using colored paper and a paper punch.

The Message

Hand each child a small handful each of black and multicolored confetti. Say: **Let's pretend the black confetti represents mean words and the bright confetti kind words. When I tell something negative a person might say, sprinkle a bit of black confetti on someone close to you. When I mention something kind, sprinkle the bright confetti. Ready? Lies** (black confetti). **Thank-you's** (bright confetti). **Gossip** (black confetti). **"I love you's"** (bright confetti). **Bad words** (black confetti). **Helpful words** (bright confetti). Say: **Look at the confetti—it's all over everyone!** Ask:

● **How is the scattered confetti like the way our words scatter to others?**

● **Can unkind words be picked up and thrown away like pieces of confetti? Explain.**

● **Why is it important to speak kindly?**

Say: **Let's read what the Bible says about the words we speak.** Ask a volunteer to read aloud 1 Thessalonians 5:11. Then say: **Kind words spoken in truth and love are the best words we can speak—and just the kind of words we want to spread to others. Our kind words encourage people in the nicest ways! Let's make a neat holder for the bright confetti to remind us of the kind words we always want to speak.**

The Meaning

Hand out the soft plastic coin purses. Let children draw faces on the fronts of the coin purses and sketch upper and lower "lips" around the openings. (See illustration.)

As you work, say: **Remember how our confetti scattered on and around our friends? That's what happens with the things we say too. Unkind words scatter hurtful feelings. But kind words scatter love. Let's pick up the pieces of black confetti and throw them away. Then we'll pick up the bright confetti and put it in your confetti cases. Then each time you say something kind to someone, scatter a bit of kindness-confetti on them!** Pick up the confetti; hand out extra confetti if you're short.

Let's close with a special Take-It-Away Card you can take home along with your Kindness Confetti Case to remind you that God wants us to speak kind words.

Take-It-Away Card

Hand Take-It-Away Card 11 to each child as you close the message time. Have one volunteer read aloud the "Point to Make" and another the "Verse to View." End by challenging children to read the card often.

> **Message 11—Kindness Confetti**
> God wants us to speak kindly.
>
> Therefore encourage one another.
> • I Thessalonians 5:11 •

Choose-n-Use Options

- Use leftover confetti to decorate kindness cups. Glue confetti to paper cups in mosaic-style. When the cups are dry, write kind words on the cups, such as "love," "peace," "joy," and "Jesus." Present the cups to another class and suggest they use them to hold pencils, pens, or little trinkets.

- Let older children cut out funny pink construction-paper mouths and tongues. Then have children read Ephesians 4:15, 29-32 and 1 Thessalonians 5:11 and list "good types of words" on their paper objects. Use words such as "truth," "encouragement," "forgiveness," and "love."

12. All Around the World

Real maps help children understand we're ambassadors for Jesus.

Point to Make: We can pray for others around the world.

Verse to View: We are therefore Christ's ambassadors.
2 Corinthians 5:20

Preparation: You'll need Tacky craft glue, scissors, blue cord, a world map or old atlas pages, a paper punch, a round plastic margarine lid for each child, and a photocopy of Take-It-Away Card 12 for each child.

Cut an 18-inch length of blue cord for each child and a circular portion of map to fit each margarine lid.

The Message

Hold up a world map or an atlas page. Invite children to identify countries and cities around the world. Say: **There are people all over the world who live in different countries, speak different languages, eat different foods, and do different things. But even though all people are different, we have something in common—the need for love and forgiveness!**

▲ **Who can give everyone in the world love and forgiveness?**

▲ **How can we help others know, love, and follow Jesus?**

Say: **In the Bible, we're told to be ambassadors for Jesus. An ambassador is a person who represents someone to another country. If we're ambassadors for Jesus, that means we help others around the world know who Jesus is. And that's a very special job! Let's make Wearable World Necklaces as we learn more about how we can help others around the world know Jesus.**

The Meaning

Hand each child a plastic lid, portion of map, and blue cord. Have children glue the maps to the lids, then use a paper punch to make a hole near the edge of each lid. Thread blue cord through the hole and tie it into a necklace loop. As you work, ask:

▲ **What are ways to represent Jesus to others?**

▲ **How can prayer help people around the world know Jesus?**

Say: **Look at the maps you're wearing and see if you recognize what part of the world they're from. We'll call this your "world prayer-portion." As special ambassadors for Jesus, let's offer a prayer for the people in your "portion of the world."** Pray: **Dear God, please help the people in this part of the world hear the good news about Jesus' love and forgiveness. Help them know, love, and follow Jesus and be ambassadors for him too. Amen. I'm challenging you ambassadors to pray for your world prayer-portion every day this week. That way, we'll be ambassadors for Jesus all around the world!**

Let's close with a special Take-It-Away Card you can take home along with your Wearable World Necklace.

Take-It-Away Card

Hand Take-It-Away Card 12 to each child as you close the message time. Have one volunteer read aloud the "Point to Make" and another the "Verse to View." End by challenging children to read the card often.

Message 12—All Around the World
We can pray for others around the world. ◄

We are therefore Christ's ambassadors. ►

▲ 2 Corinthians 5:20

Choose-n-Use Options

▲ Invite younger children to toss a plastic globe or playground ball "globe" around a circle as they sing the following words to the tune of "The Farmer in the Dell." Then toss the ball across the circle and sing "All Around the World."

All around the world! All around the world—

We can tell of Jesus' love all around the world!

▲ Provide reference books and encyclopedias for older children to look up countries included in their Wearable World Necklaces. Ask kids to read aloud their "mini-reports" and tell one way they could help someone in that part of the world know Jesus.

13. Anything Bags

Clever "seas-in-a-bag" help kids realize that God can do anything.

Point to Make: God can do anything.

Verse to View: Is anything too hard for the Lord?   Genesis 18:14

Preparation: You'll need plastic resealable sandwich bags, cornstarch, water, vegetable oil, measuring cups, clear plastic packing tape, red food coloring, and a photocopy of Take-It-Away Card 13 for each child.

No prior preparation necessary.

The Message

Ask children to name things that are impossible, such as walking to the moon, lifting a mountain, or stopping a storm. Then ask:

■ **Why aren't people able to do all things?**
■ **Does anyone have the power to do everything? Explain.**
■ **Why can God do anything?**

Say: **God is so powerful and perfect that he can do anything—no matter how impossible it seems to us. The Bible tells us wondrous things God has done, such as stopped storms, helped very old couples have babies, and even made a flaming bush that didn't burn up! Do you remember what happened in the story of Moses and the Red Sea?**
Help children recall that God parted the Red Sea to let Moses and the Israelites safely across. Then say: **Moses knew, just as we know, that God can do anything! Let's make nifty Red Seas-in-a-Bag to remind us how the Red Sea parted because God can do anything!**

The Meaning

Hand each child a resealable sandwich bag. Help each child measure and pour in 1/4 cup cornstarch, 1/4 cup water, and several drops of red food coloring. Seal the bags securely and gently knead the "Red Seas" until they're smooth. Reopen the bags and add 1/4 cup of oil to each. Reseal tightly and cover the seal with clear packing tape. Again, knead the pretend Red

Seas until they're smooth and runny. Then let children "part the waters" by setting the bags on the floor and running their fingers across the mixture. As you play, talk about God's miraculous power and how he made the waters part, made the sun stand still in the sky, created the heavens and earth, and even sent heavenly food to Moses and the Israelites. Then ask:

■ **How does it help us to know that God can do anything?**
■ **What are ways God uses his awesome power to help us?**
■ **In what ways can we thank God for his amazing power?**

Close with a prayer thanking God for his power and his mighty love. Then say: **Isn't it wonderful to serve a God who is more powerful than anyone or anything?**

Let's close with a special Take-It-Away Card you can take home along with your Red Sea-in-a-Bag.

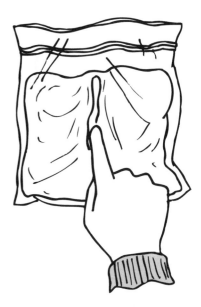

Take-It-Away Card

Hand Take-It-Away Card 13 to each child as you close the message time. Have one volunteer read aloud the "Point to Make" and another the "Verse to View." End by challenging children to read the card often.

Choose-n-Use Options

Message 13—Anything Bags
God can do anything.

Is anything too hard for the Lord?
Genesis 18:14

■ Using an old bedsheet, have younger children sit around the edges making pretend waves on the "sea." Retell various Bible stories of God's power or Jesus' power over the water as you use the sheet to make stormy waves and calm seas. Include Jesus calming the sea, Jesus walking on the water, and God parting the Red Sea.

■ Have older children form groups of three or four and each read an account of God's or Jesus' perfect power. Direct different groups to read John 11:38-44 (raising of Lazarus), John 5:1-9 (healing the lame man), John 2:1-11 (water to wine), and Exodus 10:12-15 (plague of locusts). Invite groups to act out the stories and have others guess which story is being told.

14. No Bones About It!

Clever "bones" help children realize how wondrously God made us.

Point to Make: God made us in a wonderful way.

Verse to View: I praise you because I am fearfully and wonderfully made. Psalm 139:14

Preparation: You'll need a Bible, 1/2-inch foam rubber, scissors, large paper clips, large rubber bands, and a box of Bonz doggie treats. You'll also need a photocopy of Take-It-Away Card 14 for each child.

Cut four 1-inch foam squares for each child. Make a paper clip "needle" for each child by unbending large paper clips. In addition to the foam squares, be sure you have a paper clip needle, two large paper clips, and five doggie Bonz for each child.

The Message

Have children stand, touch their toes, twist to both sides, then sit down. Ask:

● **How are our bodies able to move so well?**

● **Who decided we'd have bones, a spine, and nerves to move our bodies in different ways?**

● **Why do you think God made us so uniquely?**

Say: **Our spines help us move in different ways. In fact, each bone and nerve in our bodies was designed in special ways to help us move. We know that God made us. He gave us bones and skin and arms and heads and brains and hearts—and lots of love! Just think about how wondrously we're made! Let's see what the Bible says about the way God made us.** Read aloud Psalm 139:14. Then say: **Let's make pretend spines to remind us of how wondrously God created us.**

The Meaning

Hand each child five doggie bones, four foam squares, a large rubber band, a paper clip needle, and two other large paper clips. Demonstrate how to "thread" the rubber band loop through the needle, then poke the needle through the soft center of a doggie bone. Fasten a paper clip to the end of the rubber band to prevent it from slipping through the bone. Alternate foam squares and bones as you thread each on the rubber band. Point out how wondrously God made little cushions between our bones so they don't rub together.

After threading the last bone, add another paper clip to the end of the rubber band to hold the "spine" together. Then ask:

● **In what ways does the special way we're created show God's love for us?**

● **How can we thank God for making us so wondrously?**

Say: **Make your pretend spine bend forward, backward, and twist a bit. Each time you see your pretend spine, think of the wondrous way God has made us.**

Now let's close with a special Take-It-Away Card you can take home along with your super-spine.

Take-It-Away Card

Hand Take-It-Away Card 14 to each child as you close the message time. Have one volunteer read aloud the "Point to Make" and another the "Verse to View." End by challenging children to read the card often.

Choose-n-Use Options

Message 14—No Bones About It!
God made us in a wonderful way.

I praise you because I am fearfully and wonderfully made.

Psalm 139:14

● Sing the lively favorite "Heads and Shoulders, Knees and Toes" as you bend and point to each body part. Repeat the song several times, singing faster with each repetition.

● Let older children use the Bible to find references for things God has made. Encourage them to look in Genesis 1:1–2:4; Psalm 86:9; Psalm 95:3-5; and Psalm 104:24, 25. Have children draw pictures of their favorite things God created, then display them in a church hall for everyone to enjoy.

15. Save to Give

Simple yet colorful banks remind children to give to others.

Point to Make: God wants us to give to others.

Verse to View: It is more blessed to give than to receive. *Acts 20:35*

Preparation: You'll need a Bible, several rolls of masking tape, crayons, scissors, and a photocopy of Take-It-Away Card 15 for each child. You'll also need a clean yogurt container with lid and a shiny penny for each child.

Cut a "coin slit" in the top of each yogurt container. Invite one or two adult helpers to tear masking tape for the children at the appropriate time.

The Message

Hold up a penny. Ask:
▲ **What is money good for?**
▲ **How are people sometimes selfish with their money?**
▲ **Can money help people? Explain.**
▲ **Why do you think God wants us to share our money with others?**

Say: **God wants us to be good stewards with our money. That means that God wants us to share what we have with others who may not have as much. We can read what the Bible says about being good stewards with our money and helping others.**

Read aloud Acts 20:35, then ask:
▲ **How does helping others bring us closer to them? closer to God?**

Say: **Saving money to help those in need is important. Let's make special banks to remind us about being God's good stewards of money and generous givers of help.**

The Meaning

Hand each child a yogurt container and lid. Have children cover their containers with short pieces of masking tape. Show them how to layer and overlap the tape in different directions to completely cover the containers. When the "banks" are covered, have children use crayons to color over the tape. The crayon will be darker where the tape overlaps, creating interesting designs! As you work, ask questions such as "How can saving money help someone else?" "Who are people who might need our help?" and "How does saving, then giving to others, show our love?"

When the banks are finished, say: **We can save money to help others—and we can begin saving right now! Here's a shiny penny to drop in your banks. See how much more you can save over the next month, then choose a place to donate your savings.** Hand each child a penny.

Then say: **Let's close with a special Take-It-Away Card you can take home along with your savings bank.**

Take-It-Away Card

Hand Take-It-Away Card 15 to each child as you close the message time. Have one volunteer read aloud the "Point to Make" and another the "Verse to View." End by challenging children to read the card often.

Message 15—Save to Give
God wants us to give to others.

It is more blessed to give than to receive.

Acts 20:35

Choose-n-Use Options

▲ Lay small pieces of aluminum foil over different coins, then rub over the foil with your fingernails to make the outlines of the coins show through. Remove the coins. Tape fishing line to the foil coins and suspend them mobile-style from plastic drinking straws. Hang your creation with a sign that reads: "God wants us to save to give away, so others in need will have a good day! Give to others in love!"

▲ Challenge older kids to look up Bible verses on giving. Then have children draw piggy banks on a large sheet of poster board. Write the verses under the banks. Then hold a "Hundred-Penny Carnival" in which children each bring a hundred pennies in a bag. Toss pennies onto the game board. Pennies landing on or touching piggy banks are donated to a children's home or other cause. Pennies not landing on banks are tossed again. End with a snack of raw carrot "coins," crunchy golden "coin" crackers, and "golden" cheese cubes!

16. Creation Celebration

Darling puppets—and a lively song—let kids praise the Creator.

Point to Make: We're thankful for God's creation.

Verse to View: God saw all that he had made, and it was very good.
Genesis 1:31

Preparation: You'll need a Bible; fine-tipped permanent markers; Tacky craft glue; cotton balls; tiny silk flower buds; pairs of light, solid-color cotton gardening gloves; and a photocopy of Take-It-Away Card 16 for each child.

Purchase inexpensive cotton gardening gloves at most discount stores. You'll need one right- or left-hand glove for each child.

The Message

Say: **Think for a moment about all that's in the world, all that shines in the heavens, all that swims in the seas.** Pause for a moment, then ask:

■ **Who created the world and the heavens?**
■ **Why do you think God wanted the world to be such a beautiful place?**
■ **What are your favorite parts of God's creation? Why?**
■ **How does God's creation show his love for us?**
■ **How can we show God how much we love the world he's given us?**

Say: **We know that God is our creator and lovingly made the world. In fact, do you know what God saw when he finished creating the world?** Read aloud Genesis 1:31, then say: **God saw that his creation was very good. God was pleased, and so are we. Just think of how awful it would be if God had made only one color...or one animal...or no trees or stars! God was so wise and loving to have made our world exactly as he did. Let's thank God for his loving creation by making fun puppets and learning a special thank-you song.**

The Meaning

Hand each child a glove. Say: **What's one thing God created in the sky that we can thank him for?** Lead children to suggest clouds or the sun, then have each child use a marker to draw a bright sun on the thumb of his or her glove. Position the drawing so it's on the palm side of the glove. Glue a bit of cotton below the sun. Then have each child draw a flower on the index finger of the glove and glue on a silk flower bud. Continue by drawing an animal or animal face on the third finger, a person on the fourth finger, and a heart on the pinkie finger. Finally, help children write "Thank you, God" on the palms of the gloves.

When the gloves are complete, wear them as you sing "He's Got the Whole World in His Hands" as a thank-you song to God. Wiggle the appropriate fingers as you sing the following verses:

- ■ "He's got the sun and the clouds in his hands..."
- ■ "He's got the ferns and the flowers in his hands..."
- ■ "He's got the fuzzy-wuzzy animals in his hands..."
- ■ "He's got you and me in his hands..."
- ■ "He's got lots and lots of love in his hands..."

After singing, say: **Let's close with a special Take-It-Away Card you can take home along with your Creation Celebration glove.**

Take-It-Away Card

Hand Take-It-Away Card 16 to each child as you close the message time. Have one volunteer read aloud the "Point to Make" and another the "Verse to View." End by challenging children to read the card often.

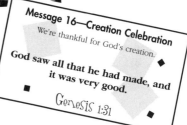

Message 16—Creation Celebration
We're thankful for God's creation.

God saw all that he had made, and it was very good.

Genesis 1:31

Choose-n-Use Options

- ■ Younger children will enjoy using their glove puppets to help tell the story of God's creation. Simply retell the story from Genesis 1 or read the story aloud from a Bible storybook. Let children hold high the appropriate fingers as you list each day of creation. When you get to the animals on day six, encourage children to make noises corresponding to the animals they've drawn.

- ■ Help older children realize the differences between people "making" things and God "creating" them. For example, point to a chair and ask how people *made* the chair. Then trace the materials and labor back to God's creations to see how God *created* the trees and the people to make the chairs. Continue with other items in the room, such as tables, books, the Bible, wastebaskets, windows, and the church building. Remind children that God is the only true creator!

17. Worship Bells

Ringy-swingy bells help children understand why we worship God.

Point to Make: We worship God for who he is and for what he does.

Verse to View: Come, let us bow down in worship.   Psalm 95:6

Preparation: You'll need a Bible, markers or paint pens, medium-size jingle bells, ribbon, scissors, and a photocopy of Take-It-Away Card 17 for each child. You'll also need one small clay flowerpot (1 1/2 to 2 inches in diameter) for each child.

Cut a 6-inch length of ribbon for each child.

The Message

Shake several jingle bells in your hands and ask:

● **What makes this sound?**
● **Why do you think a lot of churches have bells?**

Say: **Many churches ring bells to tell people it's time to worship God. But what is worship? What do we do when we worship God?** Pause for responses. **When we worship God, we tell God how special he is. We worship God for who he is and for what he does. Let's see what the Bible says about who God is.** Read aloud Psalm 93:1 and Psalm 95:1, 6. Then say: **Now let's read about what God can do.** Read aloud Psalm 93:4 and Psalm 95:3-5. **We worship God because God is all-powerful and all-loving. And we worship God because God can do anything. Let's make special bells to help us remember why we worship God—for who God is and for what God does.**

The Meaning

Hand each child a clay pot, jingle bell, and ribbon. Tell children to hold pots upside down and write the words "Who God Is . . . What God Does" around the bottom rims of the pots. Use markers or paint pens to decorate the sides of the pots. Help children thread jingle bells onto the ribbons, then tie knots in the centers of the ribbons and thread them through the holes in the pots. Be sure the jingle bells remain on the insides of the pots! Tie the ends of the ribbon to form loops to hang the bells.

As you work, ask:

- **What are words to describe who God is?**
- **What are things God has done in the Bible? in your own life?**
- **How can you worship God this week?**

Say: **Your worship bells are beautiful. Let's ring the bells and, as you do, tell God you love him with all your heart.** Pause as children ring their bells. Then say: **Let's set down the worship bells and say a prayer.** Pray: **Dear God, we love you and want to worship you. We give you honor for who you are. We give you praise for all you do. Help us look for ways to worship and thank you for your great love and power. Amen.**

Let's close with a special Take-It-Away Card you can take home along with your worship bell.

Take-It-Away Card

Hand Take-It-Away Card 17 to each child as you close the message time. Have one volunteer read aloud the "Point to Make" and another the "Verse to View." End by challenging children to read the card often.

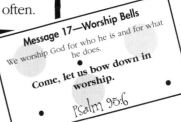

Message 17—Worship Bells
We worship God for who he is and for what he does.
●
Come, let us bow down in worship.
Psalm 95:6

Choose-n-Use Options

- Write the word "WHO" on one sheet of paper and the word "WHAT" on another. Tape the papers at opposite ends of the room. Have children stand in the center of the room. Call out descriptions of who God is or what God does and have kids hop to the correct paper. For example, if you call out, "love," have kids hop to the WHO paper. If you say, "forgives us," have kids hop to the WHAT paper.

- Challenge older children to brainstorm ways to worship God, such as through prayer, kindness, forgiveness, song, quiet reflection, and giving. Encourage children to use a concordance to look up the words "worship" and "praise" as they are used in various Psalms (33:2; 89:5; 95:6; 104:33; 109:30; 147:1). Then have children make a colorful poster of the worship verses.

18. Mission of Love

Crafty walking sticks teach children what it means to be a missionary for Jesus.

Point to Make: We're Christ's missionaries.

Verse to View: How beautiful are the feet of those who bring good news! Romans 10:15

Preparation: You'll need a Bible, colored electrical tape, craft feathers, jute or leather cord, scissors, a large stick for each child, and a photocopy of Take-It-Away Card 18 for each child.

Choose sticks that are at least 3-feet long and 1/2-inch thick. Clear any leaves, loose bark, or smaller twigs from the sticks. Cut two 2-foot lengths of jute or leather cord for each child.

The Message

Gather children and ask:
▲ **What is a mission?**
▲ **Why are some missions very important?**

Say: **A mission is something we do with a real purpose—usually to help others. When someone is on a special mission for Jesus, he or she is a missionary. But did you know that Jesus wanted you and me to be missionaries too? Let's read what Jesus said about being missionaries for him. Listen for where we're to go and what we're to do on our special mission.** Read aloud Romans 10:15. Then ask:
▲ **What is our special mission for Jesus?**
▲ **Where are we to go as missionaries for Jesus?**
▲ **How can we help others in our mission learn about Jesus?**

Say: **Being missionaries for Jesus means we're willing to go all over the world to tell others about Jesus' love and forgiveness. Some missionaries go to foreign countries, and some missionaries work right in their own neighborhoods. In Bible days, many missionaries walked miles and miles to tell others about Jesus. They used walking sticks to help them climb hills, cross streams, and walk through valleys. Let's make walking sticks to remind us of these missionaries while we learn more about the importance of being missionaries for Jesus.**

The Meaning

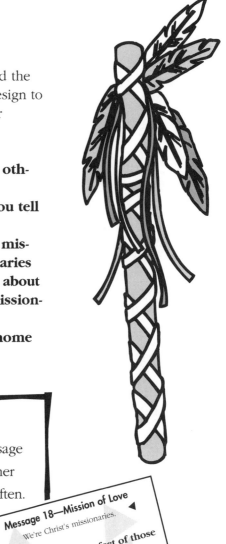

Hand each child a stick to decorate. Wrap leather or jute around the sticks, then use bits of electrical tape to add a dash of color and design to the walking sticks. Finally, let children tuck feathers into the jute or leather cord. As children work, ask:

▲ **Why is it important to be Jesus' missionaries?**

▲ **How does being a special missionary show our love for others? for Jesus?**

▲ **As a missionary in your own neighborhood, who can you tell about Jesus this week?**

Say: **Jesus gave us a special job when he chose us to be his missionaries. Let's pray and ask God's help to be the best missionaries we can be.** Pray: **Dear God, help us go into all the world to tell about Jesus' love and forgiveness. Thank you for the chance to be missionaries on a special mission of love. Amen.**

Let's close with a special Take-It-Away Card you can take home along with your missionary walking stick.

Take-It-Away Card

Hand Take-It-Away Card 18 to each child as you close the message time. Have one volunteer read aloud the "Point to Make" and another the "Verse to View." End by challenging children to read the card often.

> **Message 18—Mission of Love**
> We're Christ's missionaries.
> How beautiful are the feet of those who bring good news!
> Romans 10:15

Choose-n-Use Options

▲ Provide paper, pencils, crayons, and markers. Invite children to draw pictures for and write letters to missionaries your church supports. Encourage children to give a special thank-you to the missionaries for telling others about Jesus.

▲ Challenge older children to research Paul's missionary trips to other churches. Let children use maps in the backs of their Bibles or in Bible atlases to outline Paul's travels. Then write down verses about Paul's travels and list the churches Paul visited. Compile the work in a decorated folder and title it: "Paul's Mission of Love." Set the book in a place for everyone to read and enjoy.

19. Bee-Attitudes

Clever buzzy bees help kids learn about the Beatitudes.

Point to Make: We can live as Jesus wants us to live.

Verse to View: If we live, we live to the Lord.   Romans 14:8

Preparation: You'll need a Bible, rubber bands, chenille wires, black markers, pairs of yellow baby socks, fiberfill, black electrical tape, scissors, and photocopies of the "Bee-Attitudes" from page 106. You'll also need a photocopy of Take-It-Away Card 19 for each child.

Make a photocopy of the Bee-Attitudes from page 106 for each child. If children are young, cut out sets of pieces and put each set in an envelope. Prepare a stuffed Bee-Attitude according to the directions in this activity.

The Message

Hold up the stuffed Bee-Attitude and repeat the following riddle:
Happy, busy, buzz-along—
Making sweetness all day long!
What am I?
Say: **You're right—a busy, buzzy bumblebee! Bees are pretty wonderful and have great attitudes. They're busy and useful, happily making honey that can be shared with others. You know, bees could have different attitudes. They could be lazy or too flitty to make honey. People have different attitudes too. What are some attitudes that people have?** Lead children to mention attitudes such as teachable, willing, helpful, happy, cranky, and lazy. Then ask:
■ **Why are attitudes important?**
■ **How can attitudes affect the way we live? treat others? follow Jesus?**
Say: **Did you know that Jesus taught us to have certain attitudes? They're called the Beatitudes, and we can think of them as "attitudes for how we should be." Let's read the Beatitudes.**

Read aloud Matthew 5:3-10. Then say: **In other words, Jesus wants us to *be* humble—not braggy, to *be* comforted—not sad, to *be* meek—not mean, to *be* just and fair, to *be* merciful, to *be* pure in heart, to *be* peacemakers, and to *be* faithful. Jesus promises that, if we have these attitudes, we'll live more like Jesus wants us to live. Let's learn more about the Beatitudes as we make cute bumblebees to remind us of the way Jesus wants us to be.**

The Meaning

Hand each child a chenille wire, yellow sock, rubber band, and handful of fiberfill. Instruct kids to stuff the socks, then close the opening with the rubber band. Add two "bumblebee stripes" with black tape, then draw a face on the opposite end of the bee. Finally, twist the chenille wire around the sock to make a "head" and two "antennae." Have children tape on the paper wings and read aloud the eight Beatitudes—or ways Jesus wants us to be. Read aloud Romans 14:8, then ask:

■ **How can we have the attitudes Jesus wants us to have?**

■ **How can having these attitudes make us stronger Christians?**

Say: **Jesus gave us the Beatitudes to teach us how to live and treat others. Each is an important attitude for Christians to develop. Now let's close with a special Take-It-Away Card you can take home along with your stuffed Bee-Attitude.**

Take-It-Away Card

Hand Take-It-Away Card 19 to each child as you close the message time. Have one volunteer read aloud the "Point to Make" and another the "Verse to View." End by challenging children to read the card often.

> **Message 19—Bee-Attitudes**
> We can live as Jesus wants us to live.
>
> ■ **If we live, we live to the Lord.**
> Romans 14:8

Choose-n-Use Options

■ Invite kids to assemble a clever Beatitude beehive on a bulletin board or wall. Stack open egg cartons into a "honeycomb" beehive shape. Then cut out paper bees and position them flying around the hive. Write a Beatitude from Matthew 5:3-10 on each bee. Add the following caption: "BEE" the way JESUS wants us to be!

■ Older children will enjoy playing a game they make in class. Look up Matthew 5:3-10, then write the first half of each Beatitude on an index card and the second half on another card. Have each child write one half of each verse. Then mix up the cards and challenge kids to correctly match halves of the Beatitudes. When they're done, ask if anyone remembers an entire Beatitude without looking at the cards!

20. Follow-Me Friends

Unique stuffed pals remind kids that God is a constant companion.

Point to Make: God is with us all the time.

Verse to View: The Lord your God will be with you wherever you go. Joshua 1:9

Preparation: You'll need a Bible, duct tape, Tacky craft glue, buttons, a variety of men's neckties, newspapers, and a photocopy of Take-It-Away Card 20 for each child.

Check closets and secondhand stores for old neckties. Wide ties in wild patterns work especially well. You'll need one tie for each child.

The Message

Gather children and say: **I have a riddle for you. It's tricky, so listen carefully.**
I stay at home when it rains—boohoo—
But when it's sunny, I follow you!
What am I?

Give children hints, if needed, to arrive at the answer—a shadow. Then say: **Shadows follow us when we walk, run, or even stand in place. But shadows only follow us when there's light. I know someone who follows us all the time—night or day. Do you know who is always with us?** Invite children to tell their ideas, then say: **Let's read what the Bible says about God being with us wherever we go.** Read aloud Joshua 1:9, then ask:

● **In what ways does it help to know God is always with us?**

Say: **God is like a follow-me friend. He is there all the time to protect us, care for us, help us make good decisions, and love us. Let's make Follow-Me Friends to remind us of the way God follows us like our best loving friend.**

The Meaning

Let each child choose a necktie. Have children tape the small ends of the neckties closed, then loosely stuff wadded newspapers into the "body" of the necktie through the opening at the wide end. When the tie is gently stuffed, tape the wide end closed. Turn the neckties over and glue pairs of button "eyes" to the wide ends of the ties. As children work, discuss the places God goes with us and how God helps us by being near all the time.

When the Follow-Me Friends are finished, have children drape them over their arms or shoulders. Then say: **Wear your Follow-Me Friend everywhere you go today as you think about how God never leaves us—even for a moment. Now let's say a prayer thanking God for his constant presence.** Pray: **Dear God, thank you for loving us and wanting to be with us all the time—wherever we go. We love you too. Amen. Let's close with a special Take-It-Away Card you can take home along with your Follow-Me Friend.**

Take-It-Away Card

Hand Take-It-Away Card 20 to each child as you close the message time. Have one volunteer read aloud the "Point to Make" and another the "Verse to View." End by challenging children to read the card often.

> **Message 20—Follow-Me Friends**
> God is with us all the time.
>
> The Lord your God will be with you wherever you go.
> Joshua 1:9

Choose-n-Use Options

- Use your Follow-Me Friends to play a game of Follow the Leader. Choose one child to lead and have him or her use a Follow-Me Friend to make an action—such as swinging the tie and walking backward or twirling the necktie on the floor and hopping over it—for everyone else to imitate. Switch leaders often and continue until everyone has had a turn to lead the class.

- Cut out twenty paper footprints. Challenge children to brainstorm ways we can follow God and write each way on a footprint. Include ways such as learning God's Word, praying, obeying God's commands, loving Jesus, and helping others. When each footprint has a way to follow God, let children take turns laying the footprints on the floor in zany patterns that everyone has to follow.

21. Our Giving God

Cute finger puppets help children realize that God provides for his creation.

Point to Make: God gives us what we need.

Verse to View: My God will meet all your needs.   Philippians 4:19

Preparation: You'll need a Bible, markers, Tacky craft glue, several rubber gloves, scissors, and a photocopy of Take-It-Away Card 21 for each child. You'll also need a variety of craft scraps such as yarn, felt, feathers, ribbon, and fake fur.

Cut the fingers from the rubber gloves. You'll need one finger for each child—plus a few extra. Make two finger puppets according to the directions in this activity. Make one a "bird" and one a "puppy."

The Message

Slide the puppets on your fingers and say: **I brought a couple of pretend pets to help us learn about how God provides and cares for us. This is Puppy-Pal** (make the puppy puppet bark happily) **and this is Bitty-Bird** (make the bird "fly and tweet"). **Do any of you have pets? How do you care for your pets?** Allow children to respond, then say: **You care for your pets by giving them what they need, such as food, water, and a warm place to live. In other words, you provide for them.**

▲ **Who provides for us?**
▲ **What kinds of things does God provide for us?**
▲ **How does God's provision show his love?**

Say: **God created the world and all that lives in it. And God provides for his creation in wonderful ways. Let's read what the Bible says about God's provision.** Read aloud Philippians 4:19, then say: **God provides for animals and for people. In fact, God provides for his entire creation. Just as you provide for pets you love, God provides for people he loves—and we all know people are far more important than pets! Let's make finger pets to remind us of God's special provision of love. Then we'll learn ways we can thank God for providing for us.**

The Meaning

Hand each child a rubber glove finger and invite him or her to use markers and craft items to decorate pretend animals and pets. Use yarn for tails or hair, felt for noses or ears, and feathers for wings and "top-knots." As children work, encourage them to tell about the animals they're making and what things their "pets" might need.

When the finger puppets are finished, have children slip them on. Say: **God provides for all his creation—and all creation can praise and thank God.** Read aloud Psalm 117. Then say: **Let's learn a thank-you rhyme to thank God for all he provides. Use your puppets to make sound effects at the right time.**

**Thank you, God, for all you give
To every single thing that lives.
Dogs say, "Woof!" Cows say, "Moooo!"
Tigers roar, "We love you!"
A bird sings a song when he starts—
But we say, "Thank you" with our hearts!
Now let's close with a special Take-It-Away Card you can take home along with your finger puppet pal.**

Take-It-Away Card

Hand Take-It-Away Card 21 to each child as you close the message time. Have one volunteer read aloud the "Point to Make" and another the "Verse to View." End by challenging children to read the card often.

Message 21—Our Giving God ◄
God gives us what we need.

My God will meet all your needs. ►
Philippians 4:19

Choose-n-Use Options

▲ Play an active game of God Gives. On four separate sheets of paper, write Homes, Food, People, and Things. Tape the papers on four opposite walls. When you call out something God provides, such as "tomatoes," have kids hop to the correct category and say, "Thank you, God, for tomatoes!" Call out words such as apartments, houses, nests, friends, grandparents, teachers, trees, and mountains.

▲ Read about three important feasts of thanksgiving in the Old Testament. The feasts are the Feast of Unleavened Bread (Leviticus 23:4-8), the Feast of Firstfruits (Exodus 23:16; Leviticus 23:9-14), and the Feast of Tabernacles (Leviticus 23:33-36, 39-43). Visit about the ways God's people thanked him and the way we can thank God today.

22. Hooray for Help

Cool wrist-wraps teach kids that God wants us to help one another.

Point to Make: We can help each other.

Verse to View: Be kind and compassionate to one another.
Ephesians 4:32

Preparation: You'll need a Bible, self-adhesive Velcro dots, scissors, an old 1/2-inch-wide leather belt, and a photocopy of Take-It-Away Card 22 for each child. You'll also need several sheets of alphabet stickers.

Check closets and secondhand stores for old leather belts. You may need more than one belt if your class is large. Remove the belt buckle and cut the belt into 8-inch leather pieces. Cut one piece of leather for each child.

The Message

Gather children and ask:
- **When's a time someone helped you? How did it feel?**
- **Why do you think God wants us to help others?**

Say: **God loves us and helps us every day. And God also wants us to help others as he helps us. The Bible has many examples of people helping other people. Let's read one.** Retell or read aloud the parable of the Good Samaritan from a Bible storybook. Then ask:
- **How is helping others a way to show them our love? to show we love God?**
- **What would it be like if we didn't help others?**
- **What are ways we can help others?**

Encourage children to tell their ideas. Then say: **We can help each other make wrist-wraps to remind us of the importance of helping others as God desires.**

The Meaning

Have children form pairs or trios. Hand each child a piece of leather and a set of self-adhesive Velcro dots. Show children how to help each other measure the leather straps around their wrists, then attach the Velcro dots, one on the inside end of the strap and one on the outside of the other end so the ends attach around the wrist. As children work, read aloud Ephesians 4:32.

When the wraps are fit, say: **We know that the word "help" is spelled H-E-L-P. We can think of the word "help" as standing for the sentence, "Help Each of the Lord's People." That means we can help people who already know the Lord or people whom we can tell about the Lord. In others words, we can help everyone we meet! Let's put the letters H.E.L.P. on our wrist-wraps to remind us to Help Each of the Lord's People.**

When the letters are finished, say: **Let's close with a special Take-It-Away Card you can take home along with your wrist-wrap reminder.**

Take-It-Away Card

Hand Take-It-Away Card 22 to each child as you close the message time. Have one volunteer read aloud the "Point to Make" and another the "Verse to View." End by challenging children to read the card often.

Choose-n-Use Options

> Message 22—Hooray for Help
> We can help each other. ◆
>
> ■ Be kind and compassionate to one another.
> Ephesians 4:32

- Play a game of Helpful Dodge Ball. Form two groups and have groups stand at opposite sides of the room. Instruct children in each group to form pairs and to lock elbows. Decide which partners will help by picking up the ball and which will help by rolling the ball. Play like regular dodge ball, but partners must keep elbows locked and help each other by picking up and rolling the ball. If a pair gets tagged by a rolling ball, that pair joins the other side. Play until there are no pairs left on a side.

- Form four groups and hand each a sheet of poster board, markers, and scissors. Direct each group to cut out a giant letter using a letter from the word "HELP." Have the H group write on its giant letter ways God helps us, the E group write ways that Jesus helps us, the L group list ways we help others, and the P group write ways we help others learn about God and Jesus. Suspend the letters from a hanger, then hang the "helping mobile" in a place others can read and enjoy it.

23. 20/20 Vision

Clever optical-illusion tubes remind children that God's vision is perfect.

Point to Make: God sees everything.

Verse to View: The Lord looks down and sees all mankind.
Psalm 33:13

Preparation: You'll need a Bible, markers, a variety of stickers, a pair of eyeglasses, a cardboard tube for each child, and a photocopy of Take-It-Away Card 23 for each child.

No prior preparation necessary.

The Message

Wear the eyeglasses and ask:
- **How do eyeglasses help people's vision?**
- **What are other tools that help our vision?**

Lead children to include periscopes, microscopes, X-ray machines, and telescopes. Say: **Let's make some cool "X-ray" tubes to see if we can improve our vision.** Hand each child a cardboard tube to decorate with markers and stickers. When the tubes are done, have children hold the tubes in their left hands and look through them straight ahead. Now instruct kids to bring their right hands up beside the tubes. If kids are looking straight ahead, a "hole" will appear in the palms of their right hands!

After children have played with their pretend vision tubes, say: **Let's learn more about our ability to see and about who is able to see everything with perfect vision.**

The Meaning

Say: **When our eyes see things as well as possible, we say we have "20/20 vision"— or perfect vision. But our vision isn't really perfect because we're human. Who does have perfect vision?** Let children tell that God's vision is perfect. Read aloud Psalm 33:13, then say: **God has the ability to see everything—inside, outside, and way off into the** future. **God can see troubles we might have, and he can help us steer clear of those problems when we ask him. God even sees our thoughts and feelings. And because God sees everything, we can't hide from him. Do you remember what happened when Jonah tried to hide from God?** Invite children to retell the account of Jonah and the big fish or read the story from the Bible or a Bible storybook. Then ask:

● **In what ways can God's perfect vision help us?**
● **How can we trust God's perfect vision more?**

Say: **Look through your pretend X-ray tubes once more. We don't have perfect vision, but we're thankful that God does.**

Let's close with a special Take-It-Away Card you can take home along with your X-ray tube as a reminder that God sees everything.

Take-It-Away Card

Hand Take-It-Away Card 23 to each child as you close the message time. Have one volunteer read aloud the "Point to Make" and another the "Verse to View." End by challenging children to read the card often.

Message 23—20/20 Vision
God sees everything.

The Lord looks down and sees all mankind.
Psalm 33:13

Choose-n-Use Options

● Let children use their X-ray tubes to play a game of I Spy With My Little Eye. Have children peek at a Bible-story picture through their tubes and try to guess what the picture illustrates and then look at the entire picture. Discuss how it helps to view the "whole picture" to know what it's really about. Remind children that God's perfect vision let's him see the "whole picture" of our lives so he knows what's best for us.

● Bring in a variety of visual aids such as binoculars, a microscope, a telescope, and an X-ray. Let children explore the aids, then compare and contrast how each item increases our vision and helps us. Then discuss how God's vision needs no artificial aids and list ways God's perfect vision helps us much more than any earthly tool.

24. A "Fishy" Hello

Tactile pins teach children to greet other Christians with Jesus' love.

Point to Make: Christians stick together.

Verse to View: I thank my God every time I remember you.

Philippians 1:3

Preparation: You'll need several sheets of sandpaper, Tacky craft glue, poster board, scissors, brown crayons, small magnet disks or magnetic tape, and a photocopy of Take-It-Away Card 24 for each child.

Cut a 2-by-3-inch poster-board oval and matching sandpaper oval for each child.

The Message

As children gather, give silent greetings such as smiling, waving, or giving pats on the back. Ask:

▲ **What was I "saying" to you as you gathered?**

▲ **What are other silent ways to communicate? Act them out.**

Encourage children to act out a wink to say, "I have a secret," a crooked waggling finger for "Come here," and high fives for "Way to go!" Then say: **There are lots of ways to communicate without speaking aloud. Did you know that the first Christians had a silent greeting sign? They knew many people didn't believe in Jesus and wanted to hurt Christians. So early Christians invented a sign to greet fellow Christians. What sign do you think they used?** Invite children to tell their ideas, then say: **Because many early Christians were fishermen, they would greet each other by drawing fish shapes in the sand. This was a safe way to greet other Christians. Let's make wearable sandpaper fish to show we're Christians. Then we'll learn more about this sign and why Christians want to greet one another.**

The Meaning

Hand each child a poster-board oval and a sandpaper oval. Have children glue the sandpaper oval to the poster-board oval. Point out that the sandpaper reminds us of how early Christians would draw fish signs in the sand or carve them on sandy walls. Then, using a brown crayon, demonstrate how to draw an "ICHTHUS" (ICK-thoos) shape on a sandpaper oval. After children have drawn their fish shapes on the sandpaper ovals, have them glue magnetic disks or pieces of magnetic tape to the backs of the ovals. Hand each child another magnet and show children how to attach the Ichthus pins to their clothing like "tack pins." Then ask:

▲ **Why do you think Jesus wants us to greet other Christians?**

▲ **How does greeting Christians show them we care? show Jesus our love?**

▲ **Who is a Christian friend you could greet today?**

Say: **The fish symbol is called an "Ichthus"—can you say that? In Greek, the letters in the word *Ichthus* stand for the words "Jesus Christ, God, Son, Savior." Next time you see the fish-shaped Ichthus, you'll know it belongs to someone who loves Jesus too! Now let's close with a special Take-It-Away Card you can take home along with your Ichthus pin.**

Take-It-Away Card

Hand Take-It-Away Card 24 to each child as you close the message time. Have one volunteer read aloud the "Point to Make" and another the "Verse to View." End by challenging children to read the card often.

Message 24—A "Fishy" Hello
Christians stick together.
I thank my God every time I remember you.
Philippians 1:3

Choose-n-Use Options

▲ Make Ichthus bumper stickers by cutting white Con-Tact paper into 3-by-5-inch rectangles. Use permanent markers to draw long Ichthus fish symbols inside the rectangles. Then write the name "Jesus" inside the fish symbols. Encourage children to stick the bumper stickers to their bicycles, wagons, or notebooks. Tell kids to ask permission before putting any bumper stickers on adult vehicles!

▲ Older children might enjoy doing extra research on the Ichthus symbol and its Greek spelling. Look in Bible dictionaries for more about the greeting, then invite children to work in pairs and learn to write the word using the following Greek letters: ιχθυς. Write the Greek word on sandpaper and decorate the edges of the paper.

25. Believe-It Balloons

Colorful balloons show that faith is believing without seeing.

Point to Make: Faith is believing what we can't always see.

Verse to View: Now faith is being sure of what we hope for and certain of what we do not see.   Hebrews 11:1

Preparation: You'll need a Bible, large uninflated balloons, fine-tipped permanent markers, curling ribbon and crepe paper, scissors, tape, and a photocopy of Take-It-Away Card 25 for each child.

Curl several 2-foot lengths of curling ribbon for each child.

The Message

Gather children and say: **There is a saying that goes, "Seeing is believing." What do you think that saying means, and do you think it's true?** Allow children to tell their ideas, then say: **The Bible tells us that faith is believing without seeing. Listen to what the Bible says about faith.** Read aloud Hebrews 11:1, then ask:

■ **Why do you think it's important to have faith in things we can't see?**

■ **How does trusting God help us believe without seeing?**

Say: **Let's decorate some Believe-It Balloons to show that faith is believing what we can't always see.**

The Meaning

Hand children the uninflated balloons. Have children blow up the balloons and hold the ends as they use markers to decorate the balloons. While children still hold their balloons, say: **The Bible is full of examples in which people used faith instead of their eyes to believe. Rahab helped Joshua's spies because she believed in God even when she'd only heard of God's miracles. And Abraham believed God's promises even when he couldn't see them.**

■ **What will happen if we let our balloons go? How do you know?**

■ **What will happen after the balloons go up? How do you know?**

Say: **Let your balloons go, and we'll see if you're right!** After the balloons have "landed," say: **You knew that air would propel the balloons even though you couldn't see the air. And you knew gravity would pull the balloons to the floor even though you couldn't see the gravity. You believed in what you couldn't see, and that's what faith is all about!** Ask:

■ **In what ways does faith help draw us nearer to God?**

■ **How does having faith even when we can't see make God happy?**

■ **How can you have greater faith in God?**

Invite children to blow up the balloons and tie them off. Finish decorating the balloons by taping crepe paper streamers or curled ribbons to the knots. Then say: **Each time you look at your beautiful Believe-It Balloon, remember that faith is believing what we can't always see! Let's close with a special Take-It-Away Card you can take home along with your Believe-It Balloon.**

Take-It-Away Card

Hand Take-It-Away Card 25 to each child as you close the message time. Have one volunteer read aloud the "Point to Make" and another the "Verse to View." End by challenging children to read the card often.

Message 25—Believe-It Balloons
Faith is believing what we can't always see.
Now faith is being sure of what we hope for and certain of what we do not see.
Hebrews 11:1

Choose-n-Use Options

■ Make a Believe-It Balloon mobile. Decorate a "bouquet" of colorful balloons with markers and curled ribbon. Suspend the balloons from dowel rods or clothes hangers. Make the following poster-board sign to hang from your mobile: "We can't see the air, but we know that it's real. Faith is believing what we can't see or feel!"

■ Have older children read how Jesus revealed himself to Thomas (John 20:24-29). Discuss why Thomas felt he needed physical proof that Jesus was alive and why the other disciples believed without seeing. Discuss what Jesus meant when he said, "Blessed are those who have not seen and yet have believed" (John 20:29). End by saying a prayer asking God to help everyone have faith in God without having to see physical "proof" of his power and presence.

26. Team Jesus

Shiny "trophies" proclaim our victory in Jesus.

Point to Make: We're all winners with Jesus.

Verse to View: He [God] gives us the victory through our Lord Jesus Christ.   1 Corinthians 15:57

Preparation: You'll need a Bible, stapler, roll of heavy duty aluminum foil, trophy or award ribbon, self-adhesive star stickers, and a photocopy of Take-It-Away Card 26 for each child. You'll also need a small 3-inch wooden block for each child.

No prior preparation required.

The Message

Hold up the trophy or award ribbon and ask:

● **When's a time you were given an award, trophy, or special recognition? How did it feel?**

Say: **Did you know that we can all be part of a winning team? Listen to what the Bible says about "the good race." When you know whose team we're on, raise your hands.** Read aloud 1 Corinthians 15:57, then ask:

● **Whose winning team can we join?**

● **How does Jesus give us victory?**

● **How can we invite others to join "Jesus' team"?**

Say: **When we love Jesus and make him our leader, we're on the winning team—Jesus' team. We can have victory over sin and death and live forever as God's friends. When we follow Jesus, we are victorious! Let's make pretend trophies to show how proud and glad we are to know that we can be victorious with Jesus.**

The Meaning

Have children cover small wooden blocks with aluminum foil. Then hand each child a 2-foot piece of aluminum foil. Have children "sculpt" figures that represent how they feel

56

about being on Jesus' victory team. Suggest a clapping figure or one jumping for joy. Bend and pose the arms and legs, then position the figure on the block and staple the feet in place. Place stars around the sides of the "trophy" block. When the trophies are complete, invite children to tell about their figures and why they're posed as they are.

Place the trophies on the floor and stand in a circle around them. Say: **There's no greater joy than being on Jesus' winning team. Let's say a prayer to offer special thanks to Jesus for his love.** Pray: **Dear Lord, thank you for your great love and for the victory that can be ours through your forgiveness. We love you so much. Amen.**

Have children collect their trophies, then say: **Each time you look at your trophy, remember the joy of winning the good race with Jesus Christ. Let's close with a special Take-It-Away Card you can take home along with your trophy.**

Take-It-Away Card

Hand Take-It-Away Card 26 to each child as you close the message time. Have one volunteer read aloud the "Point to Make" and another the "Verse to View." End by challenging children to read the card often.

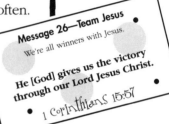

Message 26—Team Jesus
We're all winners with Jesus.

He [God] gives us the victory through our Lord Jesus Christ.
• 1 Corinthians 15:57

Choose-n-Use Options

- Make wearable "Team Jesus" blue ribbons to show others your team spirit. For each ribbon, cut a 2-inch and a 5-inch piece of 1/2-inch-wide blue ribbon. Use markers to write the word "TEAM" across the short ribbon and the word "JESUS" down the long ribbon. Make the words intersect at the letter "E." Pin the ribbons to children's shirts or dresses. Encourage children to tell others why it's great to be on Jesus' team and why we can have victory in Jesus.

- Sing the Victory Song to the tune of "Old MacDonald Had a Farm."

    V-I-C-T-O-R-Y, Jesus helps us win—

    V-I-C-T-O-R-Y, victory over sin!

    Through God's Son, we have won—

    Shout the VICTORY, ev'ryone!

    V-I-C-T-O-R-Y, Jesus helps us win!

27. Symbol of Love

Unique wearable crosses remind children that Jesus died for them.

Point to Make: Jesus died for us.

Verse to View: And he died for all. 2 Corinthians 5:15

Preparation: You'll need a Bible, thin flexible wire, scissors, leather cord, Tacky craft glue, two 3-inch-long nails and one ½-inch red felt heart for each child, and a photocopy of Take-It-Away Card 27 for each child.

Cut a 20-inch length of leather cord and two 4-inch pieces of thin wire for each child. Rub the sharp ends of the nails on cement or bricks to dull them.

The Message

Invite children to tell about a time another person took the punishment for something they did. Then ask if they ever took the blame for someone else and how they felt if they did.

Say: **Sometimes we take the blame or punishment for something someone else did. Sometimes taking the blame is a way to tell others you love them. Did you know that Jesus took the blame for things we do? Jesus loves us so much that he gave his life so our sins could be forgiven and we could live as God's friends. In other words, Jesus took the punishment for our sins.** Read aloud 2 Corinthians 5:15, then ask:

▲ **In what ways was Jesus' death a way to say he loves us?**

▲ **How do you feel knowing that Jesus died for you?**

Say: **Jesus died because he loves us and wants us to be God's friends. Jesus died because it was part of God's plan of salvation. And Jesus died so we could be forgiven from the bad things we do and say. I'm so thankful for Jesus' love! Let's make special crosses to remind us that Jesus died for us because he loves us.**

The Meaning

Hand each child two nails, two pieces of wire, a felt heart and a leather cord. Have children help each other hold the nails in a cross shape, then wrap a piece of wire around the nails in a crisscross pattern. Wrap the ends of the second piece of wire several times around the nail head at the top of the "cross" to form a loop. Slip the nail cross on the leather cord, then tie the ends of the cord to make a necklace. Glue the heart to the center of the cross.

As children work, point out that the nails remind us of the nails used at the cross where Jesus demonstrated his great love for us. Ask:

▲ **What might have happened if Jesus hadn't loved us? died for us?**

▲ **How can we thank Jesus for his love?**

Say: **Let's say a prayer thanking Jesus for his love.** Pray: **Dear God, thank you for Jesus and your loving plan of forgiveness. We're so thankful Jesus loved us enough to die for us so we can live with you. Amen.**

We can close with a special Take-It-Away Card you can take home along with your cross.

Take-It-Away Card

Hand Take-It-Away Card 27 to each child as you close the message time. Have one volunteer read aloud the "Point to Make" and another the "Verse to View." End by challenging children to read the card often.

Message 27—Symbol of Love

Jesus died for us.

And he died for all.

2 Corinthians 5:15

Choose-n-Use Options

▲ Use nails to make a clever wind chime. For each chime, dull the ends of several nails. Bend a clothes hanger into a heart shape by holding the hook and pulling the bottom center of the hanger downward. Cut varying lengths of fishing line and suspend the nails from the hanger. Use tape to keep the chimes from sliding on the hanger. Add a bow to the hook, then hang the wind chime on a porch as a "musical" reminder that Jesus loves us and died for us.

▲ Have older children form pairs and cut out two red paper hearts. Remind children that Jesus loves us and died for us. Challenge pairs to think of two other things Jesus has done or does for us, such as heals us, calms our fears, teaches us, and forgives us. Write one thing Jesus does for us on each paper heart. Then have children use Bibles and concordances to look up and write an accompanying verse on each heart. Staple the hearts into a "book" for the pastor to present to a new Christian in your church.

28. Who Is the Holy Spirit?

Simple origami doves help kids learn about the Holy Spirit.

Point to Make: The Holy Spirit helps us.

Verse to View: The Holy Spirit, whom the Father will send in my name, will teach you all things.   John 14:26

Preparation: You'll need a Bible, copy paper, scissors, and a photocopy of Take-It-Away Card 28 for each child.

Practice making folded paper doves. You may wish to draw the folding directions on poster board so children can follow along. Enlist one or two adults to help in the folding process.

The Message

Gather children and ask:
- **Who helped you learn to walk? to talk? to tie your shoes?**
- **Why is it good to have special helpers in our lives?**

Say: **The Bible tells us about a special helper and friend Jesus promised to send us. Listen as I read to you. When you know who that special helper is, clap your hands one time.** Read aloud John 14:26, then ask:
- **Who did Jesus send as our special helper and friend?**
- **How does the Holy Spirit help us?**

Say: **The Holy Spirit helps us do things Jesus would do if he were physically here. In other words, Jesus sent us the Holy Spirit so we could become Jesus' helping hands! The Holy Spirit helps us pray, be kind to others, tell others about Jesus, learn about God, and even understand the Bible better. What a wonderful friend the Holy Spirit is! Did you know that the Holy Spirit is sometimes shown as a dove in the Bible?**
Read aloud Mark 1:10. Then say: **Let's fold pretty paper doves to remind us that the Holy Spirit is our special helper and friend.**

The Meaning

Hand each child a piece of white copy paper. Use the folding diagrams and demonstrate, in a show-and-follow technique, how to fold and cut the paper dove. Have adult volunteers help children. As you fold the doves, say: **Just as we're helping you fold the paper doves and showing you the right way to do things, the Holy Spirit comes to help us and show us the right things to do as Christians.**

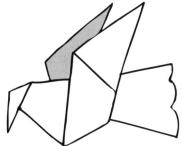

When the doves are finished, let children "fly" them around the room. Then have children form a circle and say: **Let's go around the circle. When it's your turn, hold your dove high and tell one thing the Holy Spirit can help you do this week.** Encourage children to name things such as read the Bible, tell a neighbor about Jesus, or pray. Then say: **I'm so glad that Jesus sent us such a special helper and friend. With the Holy Spirit's help, we can be special helpers and friends to others too! Let's close with a special Take-It-Away Card you can take home along with your paper dove.**

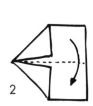
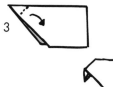

Take-It-Away Card

Hand Take-It-Away Card 28 to each child as you close the message time. Have one volunteer read aloud the "Point to Make" and another the "Verse to View." End by challenging children to read the card often.

Message 28—Who Is the Holy Spirit?
The Holy Spirit helps us.
The Holy Spirit, whom the Father will send in my name, will teach you all things.
John 14:26

Choose-n-Use Options

■ Form four groups and have each read one of these descriptions for the Holy Spirit: Mark 1:10 (dove); John 7:38, 39 (living water or streams); John 14:26 (Counselor); and Acts 2:2, 3 (fire and wind). Challenge groups to brainstorm ways to act out the descriptions. After each group has pantomimed its description, discuss why the descriptions are good symbols for the Holy Spirit.

29. Near to God

Fun figures that really move teach kids about drawing near to God.

Point to Make: We can be closer to God.

Verse to View: Come near to God and he will come near to you.

James 4:8

Preparation: You'll need a Bible, construction paper, markers, large paper clips, copy paper, a small magnet for each child, clear tape, and a photocopy of Take-It-Away Card 29 for each child.

Make a paper clip "bee" by following the directions in this activity. Draw several colorful flowers on a piece of paper. Practice making the bee "fly" from flower to flower by dragging a magnet behind the paper.

The Message

Make the paper clip bee "fly" to a flower on your drawing. Ask:
● **What draws bees close to flowers?**
● **What might happen if bees never went near flowers?**
● **What might happen if we weren't close to God?**

Set down the bee and say: **Bees draw near to flowers because flowers provide what bees need to live. We draw near to God because he has what we need to live too. But we draw near to God for other reasons. What are some reasons we want to be close to God?** Invite children to tell their ideas. Then hand each child a small magnet and a paper clip. Let kids draw the paper clip to the magnet. Then say: **See how the paper clip draws close to the magnet? God wants us to draw near to him so he can teach us, love us, protect us, and help us know his Son, Jesus. God wants us near him because he loves us—and because we love God, we want to be near him too. Do you know the best part? When we draw near to God, he draws near to us!** Read aloud James 4:8.

Say: **Let's make buzzy bees with magnets to remind us to draw near to God so he will draw near to us.**

The Meaning

Hand each child a piece of copy paper. Tear black construction-paper "bee bodies" and tape them to the large paper clips. Tape torn paper "wings" to the bees and add bits of yellow paper for stripes. Have children draw several flowers on their papers, then make their bees fly to the flowers by dragging magnets behind their papers. Ask:

- **What are ways we can draw near to God?**
- **Why is it good when God draws near to us?**
- **How can you be closer to God this week?**

Say: **We love God and want to keep growing closer to him. Each time you play with your magnetic bee or see a real bee drawing near to a flower, remember how God wants us to draw near to him—and will draw near to us! Let's close with a special Take-It-Away Card you can take home along with your buzzy bee.**

Take-It-Away Card

Hand Take-It-Away Card 29 to each child as you close the message time. Have one volunteer read aloud the "Point to Make" and another the "Verse to View." End by challenging children to read the card often.

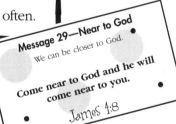

Message 29—Near to God
We can be closer to God.

Come near to God and he will come near to you.

James 4:8

Choose-n-Use Options

- Let children form pairs or trios and play a game similar to Pick-Up Sticks. Drop a handful of paper clips on a tabletop or the floor, then take turns using magnets to pick up one clip at a time. If you pick up more than one clip, return the clips to the pile and go on to the next person. Play until all the clips have been picked up.

- Hand small groups of older children pieces of paper and markers. Assign each group a different Bible character such as David, Noah, Peter, or Moses. Have children write down ways each of these people drew near to God or Jesus. Include ways such as through prayer, worship, praising God, or trusting God. Discuss how we can use the same ways to draw near to God and Jesus today.

30. God's Armor

Lively light-switch plates remind kids to put on
God's protection day and night.

Point to Make: We can put on God's protection every day.

Verse to View: Put on the full armor of God.   Ephesians 6:11

Preparation: You'll need a Bible, aluminum foil, Tacky craft glue, silver paint pens, a plastic light-switch plate for each child (plus one extra), and a photocopy of Take-It-Away Card 30 for each child.

Prepare a sample Armor of God light-switch plate according to the directions in this activity. Let it dry at least one hour.

The Message

Say: **I have a riddle for you. See if you can guess the answer.
Put me on every morning when the sun shines bright.
Wear me in the nighttime when you turn out the light.
What am I?**
Allow children to tell their guesses, which may include everything from glow-in-the-dark wristwatches to retainers for teeth to toothpaste! Then say: **This riddle has quite a few answers, but the most important one is found in the Bible.** Read aloud Ephesians 6:13-17, then ask:

▲ **What is God's armor?**

▲ **What does God's special armor do for us?**

Say: **God's special armor isn't clanky or made of metal—but it covers us with strength and protection much better than any metal suit of armor! And we can wear God's armor day and night. God's armor is made up of different pieces that help us fight the good fight with truth, peace, and God's Word. Let's read about the pieces of God's armor.** Read aloud Ephesians 6:10-17 and discuss what each piece in God's armor does for us. Then ask:

▲ **What might happen if we don't cover ourselves with God's armor?**

▲ **How can God's armor help us every day and night?**

Say: **Let's make Armor of God light-switch plates to remind us that God's armor protects us in the light and in the dark.**

▲ **64**

The Meaning

Hand each child a light-switch plate and a piece of aluminum foil. Say: **These light-switch plates remind us of one part of God's armor—the shield of faith. See how they look like shields? And they protect the wall like a shield against fingerprints. Now let's add a shiny "belt of truth."** Tear small strips of foil and glue one across the center of each light-switch plate. **Now tear out two small heart shapes. One will be the "helmet of salvation" and the other the "breastplate of righteousness."** Glue the hearts beside each other at the top of the plate directly above the light-switch hole. **Now let's add a silver letter P for the "gospel of peace."** Use the silver paint pen to make a P on the bottom half of each plate. **Finally, tear out a foil sword, which is the "sword of the Spirit"—the Bible.** Glue the sword on the belt. **Now we have shiny reminders of God's armor. Have an adult help you put the light-switch plate on your bedroom wall and remember to put on God's full armor each time you turn your lights on or off. Let's close with a special Take-It-Away Card you can take home along with your Armor of God light-switch plate.**

Take-It-Away Card

Hand Take-It-Away Card 30 to each child as you close the message time. Have one volunteer read aloud the "Point to Make" and another the "Verse to View." End by challenging children to read the card often.

> **Message 30—God's Armor**
> We can put on God's protection every day.
>
> **Put on the full armor of God.**
> ◄ Ephesians 6:11 ►

Choose-n-Use Options

▲ Have a fun relay by setting the following items at one end of the room: a belt (belt of truth), a vest (breastplate of righteousness), the Bible (sword of the Spirit), shoes (gospel of peace), a cap (helmet of salvation), and a newspaper (shield of faith). Line kids at the other end of the room. Take turns hopping to the items and selecting one to put on or hold. Tell the name of the pretend piece of God's armor, then remove it and hop back to the starting place. Continue until everyone has put on at least two different pieces of "armor."

▲ Make neat life-size soldiers of God. Have children draw or trace each other's outlines on 5-foot sections of white shelf paper. Color in the outlines and "dress" the soliders in God's full armor. Use aluminum foil and silver paint to embellish the characters. When the soldiers are finished, hang them on a wall with the verse: "Put on the full armor of God." Ephesians 6:11.

31. Wobbly Walkers

Zany "walkers" show kids that Jesus is the straight path to God.

Point to Make: Jesus is the only path to God.

Verse to View: No one comes to the Father except through me.
John 14:6

Preparation: You'll need a Bible, colored tissue paper, markers, scissors, masking tape, a lemon, a small orange for each child, and a photocopy of Take-It-Away Card 31 for each child.

Cut a 6-inch tissue paper square for each child (plus one extra). Use the extra square to make a Wobbly Walker according to the instructions in this activity.

The Message

Stick a 3-foot length of masking tape on the floor and say: **This tape represents a straight path—no twists, no turns, no goofy wobbles. I have a friend who wants to walk this straight path. Let's see if he can do it.** Place the lemon under your tissue paper Wobbly Walker and roll it down the masking tape line. It will wibble-wobble off the line in no time! Invite children to roll the Wobbly Walker down the line, then ask:

■ **How is following a winding path sometimes harder than following a straight one?**
■ **Which path is safer: a straight path or a winding one? Explain.**

Say: **The Bible tells us that the straight path to God is through Jesus. What do you think this means?** Allow children to answer, then say: **Staying on the straight path to God means knowing, loving, and following Jesus. And Jesus' straight path to God is not** *only* **the safest path, it's the only path to God! Listen to what Jesus says about the way to God, our Father.** Read aloud John 14:6, then roll the Wobbly Walker again and ask:

■ **What are things that may make us "wobble off" the straight path?**
■ **How is a straight path to God better than a crooked one?**
■ **Why do you think Jesus wants us to stay on the straight path to God?**

Say: **Let's make Wobbly Walkers to remind us how important the straight path to God is. Then we'll learn how Jesus helps us stay on that straight path.**

The Meaning

Hand each child a tissue paper square and invite children to decorate the squares like "bugs," using your Wobbly Walker as a sample. Demonstrate how to twist the four corners of the tissue paper to make "legs." Use markers to write the word "Jesus" on the oranges, then gently mold the Wobbly Walkers over the oranges. As you work, ask:

■ **How can Jesus help us stay on the straight path to God?**

■ **In what ways can we help others stay on the straight path?**

Say: **We know that the only path to God is through Jesus. Praying, reading the Bible, and following Jesus can put us on the safe, straight path to God! Now roll your Wobbly Walkers and see if their path is straighter.** The Wobbly Walkers should roll straighter with the oranges under them. Say: **Let's close with a special Take-It-Away Card you can take home along with your Wobbly Walker to remind you that Jesus is the straight path to God.**

Take-It-Away Card

Hand Take-It-Away Card 31 to each child as you close the message time. Have one volunteer read aloud the "Point to Make" and another the "Verse to View." End by challenging children to read the card often.

Message 31—Wobbly Walkers

Jesus is the only path to God. ◆

No one comes to the Father except through me.

John 14:6

Choose-n-Use Options

■ Have Wobbly Walker Race Day. Invite another class to make Wobbly Walkers, then place several masking tape lines on the floor and have pairs of kids "race" their Walkers down the lines. When everyone has raced at least three times, gather kids for "finish line" treats of orange slices and chocolate cookie "tires." As children nibble, discuss how Jesus helps us stay on the straight path to God even though we sometimes "wobble" a bit. End by sharing a prayer thanking Jesus for being the only pathway to God.

■ Have children read aloud John 14:6 and list the three ways Jesus describes himself (way, truth, and life). Then have children cut a 20-foot length of shelf paper and attach it to a hallway as a "path." Write "Travel life with Jesus—He is the . . ." in glitter at one end and the word "God" at the other end. Write the words "way," "truth," and "life" along the path. Encourage children and adults to "travel" the path to remind them that Jesus is the only pathway to God.

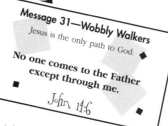

32. Meet-n-Treat

Slick stick-people help kids nurture sensitivity for others.

Point to Make: Treat others as you would treat Jesus.

Verse to View: Whatever you did for one of the least of these brothers of mine, you did for me.   Matthew 25:40

Preparation: You'll need craft sticks, markers, glue sticks, scissors, wallpaper, magazines, and a photocopy of Take-It-Away Card 32 for each child.

Cut out magazine pictures of people's heads and faces. The pictures need to be about 1 inch in size and include an ethnic variety. Cut out one picture for each child (plus one extra). Make a stick-puppet person according to the directions in this activity.

The Message

Gather children and tell them to make two fists. Say: **In your fists, you have pretend money—lots of money, all your money. Now think about the people you love most. Is it your parents? Maybe your brother or sister or grandparents? Would you give all your money to them if they needed it?** Pause for responses. **Would you give all your money to your best friend if he or she needed it?** Pause for responses. **Would you give all your money to the kid at school no one seems to like?** Encourage kids to explain their answers. Then hold up the stick-puppet person and ask:

● **Would you give all your money to this person if he or she needed it? to Jesus if he needed it? Explain.**

● **How is the way we treat Jesus different from the way we treat people we don't know?**

● **Why do you think some people only help those people they know and love?**

Say: **Jesus said, "Whatever you did to the least of these people, you did to me." What do you think he meant?** After children tell their ideas, say: **It's easier to be kind to people we know, but Jesus wants us to be kind to everyone** (hold up the puppet)—**even people we don't know. In fact, we can treat others the same way we'd treat Jesus if we met him on the street. Let's make stick-puppet people and learn more about treating others as we'd treat Jesus.**

The Meaning

Hand each child a craft stick. Let children choose magazine "faces" to glue on the tops of the sticks. Invite children to make paper clothes from wallpaper and "dress" their puppets. Write "Matthew 25:40" on the backs of the craft sticks. When the stick-puppet people are complete, hold them up and ask:

● **What are ways we can treat all people the way we'd treat Jesus?**
● **How does treating others kindly show our love for them? for Jesus?**

Say: **When we treat people we don't know with love and kindness, we're treating Jesus with love and kindness. Whatever we do for someone else, we do for Jesus. Even though you don't know the person on your puppet, you can pray for that person this week—and in that way tell Jesus you love him. Now let's close with a special Take-It-Away Card you can take home along with your stick-puppet person.**

Take-It-Away Card

Hand Take-It-Away Card 32 to each child as you close the message time. Have one volunteer read aloud the "Point to Make" and another the "Verse to View." End by challenging children to read the card often.

Message 32—Meet-n-Treat
Treat others as you would treat Jesus.
Whatever you did for one of the least of these brothers of mine, you did for me.
Matthew 25:40

Choose-n-Use Options

● Encourage children to make up "lives" for their stick-puppet people. Have children tell their puppets' names, what they like to eat, who is in their families, and their hobbies. Then tell reasons why Jesus loves their people and ways they can love them too.

● Have older children form small groups and read Matthew 5:44-48. Have children talk about why it's easier to love people we know than people who are "hard-to-love," such as people from other countries, sick people, and people who hurt others. Ask children what allowed Jesus to love even hard-to-love people such as lepers and why he wants us to do the same. Challenge children to share prayers asking Jesus' help in loving hard-to-love people as well as easy-to-love friends and family.

33. Our Special Names

Cool ID name-chains identify children as Christ's kids.

Point to Make: Jesus knows our names.

Verse to View: He calls his own sheep by name. *John 10:3*

Preparation: You'll need a Bible, scissors, aluminum pie pans, paper clips, a paper punch, thin silver cord, and a photocopy of Take-It-Away Card 33 for each child.

Cut silver cord into 20-inch lengths, one for each child. Cut the rim from a pie pan. Then cut a 1 1/2-by-2 1/2-inch aluminum rectangle for each child. Snip the corners of the rectangles to make octagons. Use scissors or pliers to slightly bend back each side of the octagons.

The Message

Ask children to tell the first names of those they know in the group. Then say: **Names are pretty special. They let people know who we are and how to tell us apart from other people. But sometimes names are hard to remember—especially if you're in a big crowd. Did you know there's someone who knows the name of every Christian in the world? Who do you think that is?** Let children tell their answers, then say: **The Bible tells us that Jesus knows the names of each of his sheep. That means Jesus knows the names of every person who loves him. Let's hear what the Bible says about Jesus knowing our names.** Read aloud John 10:3, then ask:

▲ **How does it feel to know that Jesus knows your special name?**

▲ **How does Jesus knowing our names show his love for us?**

Say: **Jesus knows us because he loves us. Let's make name-chains to remind us that Jesus knows our names. Then we'll learn what other things Jesus knows about us.**

The Meaning

Hand each child an aluminum octagon, a piece of silver cord, and a paper clip. Demonstrate how to place the octagon on a soft surface such as the carpet or a soft book. Have each child use the paper clip to "carve" the initial of his or her first name onto the aluminum.

Use the paper punch to make a hole in the top of each "ID tag," then thread the silver cord through the hole. Tie the ends in a knot and wear the name-chain as a necklace. Ask:

▲ **What other things does Jesus know about us?**

▲ **Why do you think Jesus knows so much about us?**

Say: **Because Jesus loves us so much, he wants to know everything about us—such as when we're happy or sad, what our dreams are, and even what our favorite flavor of ice cream is! We're special to Jesus, and he calls each of us by name. Wear your special ID tag to remind yourself how special you are to Jesus—and how he always calls your name in love!**

Let's close with a special Take-It-Away Card you can take home along with your name-chain ID tag.

Take-It-Away Card

Hand Take-It-Away Card 33 to each child as you close the message time. Have one volunteer read aloud the "Point to Make" and another the "Verse to View." End by challenging children to read the card often.

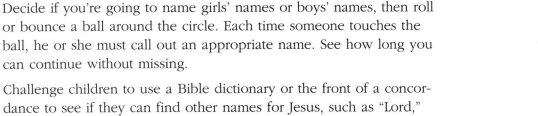

Message 33—Our Special Names
◄ Jesus knows our names. ◄
He calls his own sheep by name. ►
▲ John 10:3

Choose-n-Use Options

▲ Play the Name Game. Begin by forming a sitting or standing circle. Decide if you're going to name girls' names or boys' names, then roll or bounce a ball around the circle. Each time someone touches the ball, he or she must call out an appropriate name. See how long you can continue without missing.

▲ Challenge children to use a Bible dictionary or the front of a concordance to see if they can find other names for Jesus, such as "Lord," "Emmanuel," and "Christ." Then see what descriptive names kids can find, such as "Lamb of God," "Bread of Life," and "Lion of Judah." You may wish to cooperatively create a poster of Jesus' names and title it: "We Call Him Jesus—We Call Him Love!"

34. Focus of Faith

Color-scopes remind children to focus on Jesus.

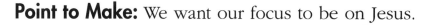

Point to Make: We want our focus to be on Jesus.

Verse to View: Let us fix our eyes on Jesus.   Hebrews 12:2

Preparation: You'll need a Bible, cardboard tubes, markers, clear plastic wrap, yellow construction paper, metallic confetti, clear packing tape, scissors, and a photocopy of Take-It-Away Card 34 for each child.

Purchase metallic confetti shapes such as hearts in party stores or gift wrapping departments. Cut a 1/2-inch-tall yellow paper cross for each child.

The Message

Secretly ask one child to distract the others with hand motions or whispering as you introduce the message time. As the child begins distracting, say: **Today we're going to be talking about keeping our focus where it's most important. And that isn't always as easy as it seems. Peter found that out one day on a boat.** Pause for a moment, then ask children to repeat what you'll be learning today. Let children respond, then halt the "distracter." Ask:

■ **Why was it difficult to hear what I was saying?**

■ **How do distractions keep us from focusing?**

■ **Why is it important to keep our focus on Jesus even though things try to distract us?**

Say: **Peter learned the importance of keeping his focus on Jesus. Let's read about that time.** Read aloud Matthew 14:22-31, then ask:

■ **What happened when Peter took his focus off Jesus?**

■ **What can happen if we take our focus from Jesus?**

■ **How does keeping our focus on Jesus strengthen our faith? bring us nearer Jesus?**

Say: **We can make colorful Focus of Faith Tubes to remind us to focus on Jesus. Then we'll learn how to focus more on Jesus every day.**

The Meaning

Give each child a cardboard tube. Have children work in pairs and each tear two 4-inch squares of clear plastic wrap. Tape one piece of plastic over one end of each tube, stretching it tightly and taping the wrap to the tube. Next, sprinkle about a tablespoon of metallic confetti on top of the plastic and place a yellow paper cross in the confetti. Loosely tape the second piece of plastic wrap over the confetti and tape it to the tube. Use markers to decorate the tubes.

As you work, discuss ways to keep our focus on Jesus, such as reading the Bible and praying. When the tubes are finished, invite children to point them at a light or window and peek through them. Have children focus on the cross as you say: **The Bible tells us to "fix our eyes on Jesus." Keeping our focus on Jesus helps us stay close to Jesus and his love. Even when things try to distract us, it's important to focus on Jesus. Let's close with a special Take-It-Away Card you can take home along with your Focus of Faith Tube.**

Take-It-Away Card

Hand Take-It-Away Card 34 to each child as you close the message time. Have one volunteer read aloud the "Point to Make" and another the "Verse to View." End by challenging children to read the card often.

Choose-n-Use Options

Message 34—Focus of Faith
We want our focus to be on Jesus.

Let us fix our eyes on Jesus.
Hebrews 12:2

■ Punch holes in the centers of two index cards. Have children form two groups. Hand an index card to a child in each group and have them cover their eyes. Hold up a Bible picture with Jesus as a part of the illustration. Challenge the pair to identify the picture by focusing their eyesight through the holes in the cards. The first child to focus on Jesus says, "Jesus is my focus of faith!" Then that child can choose the next picture.

■ Have children form two lines facing each other and about 2 feet apart. Choose a child from each line to hold a plastic spoon with a hard-boiled egg balanced on it. Have the "egg-walkers" start from opposite ends of the lines and try to walk between the groups as children try to distract them. When everyone has had a chance to walk the "focus walk," discuss what things distract our focus from Jesus and how we can direct our focus back to Jesus.

35. Step by Step

Roll-around "Trust Steppers" remind children that
we trust Jesus more every day.

Point to Make: Trusting Jesus comes step by step.

Verse to View: Trust in God; trust also in me.   John 14:1

Preparation: You'll need a Bible, paper plates, scissors, plastic margarine lids, brass paper fasteners, dowel rods, markers, tape, pinking shears, construction paper, and a photocopy of Take-It-Away Card 35 for each child.

Cut the edges from paper plates. Use pinking shears to cut around the edges of plastic lids to give them jagged edges. Prepare one lid for each child. Make a "Trust Stepper" according to the directions in this activity. You'll need a 2-foot dowel rod for each Trust Stepper.

The Message

Place the craft items several feet away from children. Ask children to invent ways to travel to the items, such as on tiptoes, walking backward, crawling, or hopping. When everyone is beside the craft materials, ask:

● **Why couldn't one giant step have gotten you where you needed to go?**

● **In what ways does taking things in small steps help you reach a goal?**

● **How does taking many small steps help you reach your goal more safely than taking big steps?**

Roll your Trust Stepper slowly back and forth by the children and say: **Sometimes we need to do things in small steps—such as learning to walk or read. If we take too big a step, we might fall or not learn something well. Did you know trust is something that grows little by little, step by step? Each time we trust Jesus, we learn to trust him more! Listen to what the Bible says about trust.** Read aloud John 14:1. Then ask:

● **How does trusting Jesus in small ways help our trust grow bigger?**

● **Why do you think it's important to trust Jesus more each day?**

Say: **When we trust Jesus a little more each day, we soon have giant trust—and that's just what Jesus wants us to have! When we trust Jesus, we're able to make better decisions, love others more, and even love God more. Trusting Jesus helps us not to be afraid and to turn to Jesus when we have troubles. So let's make cool Trust Steppers to remind us that growing faith in Jesus comes step by step.**

The Meaning

Hand each child a paper plate. Have children tear out giant paper noses and tape them to one side of their plates to make "profiles." Use markers to draw faces and add construction-paper hair, glasses, or other fun features. Have children tear four small paper "feet" and tape them to a plastic lid. Then help children attach the paper plates to the lids with paper fasteners. (See illustration.) Securely tape a dowel rod to the back of each plate as a handle. Then invite children to take their Trust Steppers for a "walk" by holding the handle and gently pushing the Steppers along the carpet. The feet will turn and appear to be taking little steps! Then gather everyone and ask:

● **How can we trust Jesus more each day?**

● **How can we help someone else trust Jesus step by step?**

Say: **Just as we learned to walk in small steps before we could run, we learn to trust Jesus in small steps—then we trust him with all our lives!**

Let's close with a special Take-It-Away Card you can take home along with your Trust Stepper.

Take-It-Away Card

Hand Take-It-Away Card 35 to each child as you close the message time. Have one volunteer read aloud the "Point to Make" and another the "Verse to View." End by challenging children to read the card often.

> **Message 35—Step by Step**
> Trusting Jesus comes step by step.
>
> **Trust in God; trust also in me.**
> John 14:1

Choose-n-Use Options

● Take your Trust Steppers on a walk outside. As you roll along, visit about the other things we learn to do in small steps, such as hop, talk, and ride bicycles. Point out that without learning some things in small steps, we'd never be able to do them. Explain that trusting Jesus—even loving him and putting our faith in him—all come step by step. End your walk with a prayer asking Jesus to help your trust in him grow more each day.

● Have children brainstorm aspects of faith that tend to grow in small steps, such as love, joy, belief, hope, peace, faith, and trust. Write each on a brown paper "stepping-stone," then tape the stones close together across the floor. Have children step across the stones, then tape them a bit farther apart. Continue taking bigger steps and seeing how far you can travel across the room. Point out how small the steps were to begin with but how big they are now!

36. Mold Me, God

Snappy Pencil-Toppers remind kids that God molds us as he chooses.

Point to Make: God molds us as he desires.

Verse to View: We are the clay, you are the potter.   Isaiah 64:8

Preparation: You'll need a Bible, unsharpened pencils, one kneadable eraser for each child, scissors, paper clips, and a photocopy of Take-It-Away Card 36 for each child.

Purchase kneadable erasers from most art supply stores. Cut each eraser in half. If you can't find these neat moldable erasers, use a walnut-size piece of clay for each child.

The Message

Choose two children to be Live Statues and two children to be Silly Sculptors. Have the Silly Sculptors pose their make-believe statues into foods such as flat pancakes or roly-poly apples. Invite the rest of the children to guess what foods have been molded. Then have kids return to their places and ask:

▲ **What does it mean to sculpt—or mold—something into a particular shape?**

▲ **What are things that might be molded, sculpted, or formed?**

▲ **How does something that's molded become changed from its original form?**

Say: **A sculptor or potter molds things from clay so the pieces take on the shape of what the potter desires. Did you know that the Bible talks about clay and a potter? Listen.** Read aloud Isaiah 64:8, then ask:

▲ **Who is the potter? Who is the clay?**

▲ **Why do you think God wants to mold us as he desires?**

▲ **Why is it better for us to be like clay instead of like rocks?**

Say: **God wants us to become all he desires—and God helps us do that by molding and shaping us with his love. It's important to remember that we need to be pliable and moldable like clay so that God can shape us as he desires. Let's mold figures to go on pencil tops to remind us that we're like clay in the potter's—God's—hands.**

The Meaning

Hand each child an unsharpened pencil and two eraser halves (or chunk of self-hardening clay). Have children wrap one piece of their kneadable eraser (or half of the clay) around the eraser end of a pencil and pinch together the sides and top. Smooth the kneadable eraser to make a "head." Pull off small bits from the second half of the eraser and stick them on as ears or noses. Use paper clips to form eyes, hair, freckles, or other features. Point out how the eraser has changed in the shaping process—just as we become changed when God shapes us. Ask children what they think God molds us to be—for example, loving, forgiving, and full of faith.

Say: **Your Pencil-Toppers look so cute and so different from the lumps we started with. That's a lot like how we are when God shapes us. We go from "lumps of clay" to being the people God desires us to be! Let's close with a special Take-It-Away Card you can take home along with your Pencil-Topper.**

Take-It-Away Card

Hand Take-It-Away Card 36 to each child as you close the message time. Have one volunteer read aloud the "Point to Make" and another the "Verse to View." End by challenging children to read the card often.

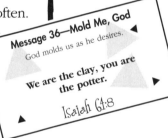

Message 36—Mold Me, God
God molds us as he desires.

We are the clay, you are the potter.

Isaiah 64:8

Choose-n-Use Options

▲ Have children form trios and choose one person to be the sculptor while the other two will be clay. Challenge children to think of one attribute God wants us to have, such as being kind. Then have the sculptor pose—or "sculpt"—the clay into that shape. For example, one person helping another who has fallen might represent kindness. Let the rest of the class guess what's been sculpted. For more fun, sculpt figures out of crinkled aluminum foil or chenille wires.

▲ Hang a large sheet of paper on the wall and divide the paper in half, with one side titled "Then we were..." and the other side titled "But now we are..." Challenge children to brainstorm ways we become changed by God's touch. For example, the sides might read, "Then we were mean" and "But now we are caring" or "Then we were selfish" and "But now we are sharing." When you're finished, read each side, then offer a prayer thanking God for being such a loving potter and changing us to be the people he chooses.

37. Prayer Fingers

Zany inflatable fingers teach children the power of prayer.

Point to Make: There is God's power in prayer.

Verse to View: The prayer of a righteous man is powerful and effective. James 5:16

Preparation: You'll need a Bible, fine-tipped permanent markers, a pair of latex gloves for each child, curling ribbon, scissors, double-sided carpet tape, and a photocopy of Take-It-Away Card 37 for each child.

Gently wipe the latex gloves with a damp cloth to remove any latex powder (or use hypoallergenic latex gloves). Ask adult volunteers to help tie off the gloves like balloons during the message time.

The Message

Say: **We all know that prayer is when we talk to God. But how do we pray and what does prayer do? Look at your fingers. Just as fingers help us accomplish things, so does prayer. We'll make cool Prayer Fingers during the message time to teach us about the power of prayer.**

Hand each child a pair of latex gloves and a marker. Have kids write the meaning of each Finger of Prayer on the fingers of their gloves as you go through them in the following section.

The Meaning

On the thumb of one glove, write the words "Hello, God." This is the finger that tells us to begin prayer by greeting God. On the second finger, write "praise" and remember to praise God for who he is. On the third finger, write "needs" and remember to pray for what you or others need. Write "thank you" on the next finger so you always thank God for his blessings. On the last finger, write "Jesus" and remember to pray in Jesus' name.

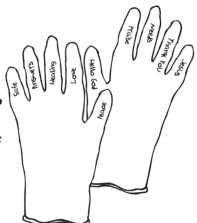

On the thumb of the other glove, write "peace," which God promises if we give our troubles to him. On the next finger, write "love," which God gives us through prayer. Write "healing" on the third finger. God heals our hurts and hurt feelings when we pray. On the next finger, write "answers," which is what God promises to do with our prayers—but in his time and in his way. And on the last finger, write "safe," which means that God protects us when we pray to him.

Show kids how to use bits of double-sided tape to tape the fingers together to make "prayer-hands," with the writing facing out. Then gently inflate the gloves to make 3-D hands. Have adults help knot the wrists of each glove, then tie the knots together with ribbon. Say: **Prayer isn't just about talking to God—it's about using the power God gives us through prayer. And that power includes protection, healing, loving others, thanking God, and praising God for who he is!** Read aloud James 5:16, then say: **Let's close with a special Take-It-Away Card you can take home along with your Prayer Fingers to remind you of the power there is in praying.**

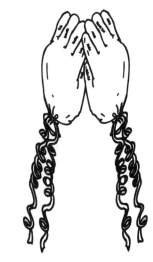

Take-It-Away Card

Hand Take-It-Away Card 37 to each child as you close the message time. Have one volunteer read aloud the "Point to Make" and another the "Verse to View." End by challenging children to read the card often.

Choose-n-Use Options

> **Message 37—Prayer Fingers**
> There is God's power in prayer. ◆
>
> The prayer of a righteous man is powerful and effective.
>
> James 5:16

■ Sit in a circle and pass two sets of the "prayer hands." When the leader says "stop," have the children holding the hands each name one of the ten fingers of prayer. Let a child on either side read the fingers to confirm the answer. Then continue passing the bouncy hands. If you have an extra glove, blow it up like a balloon and bop it around the circle as you name good things that come from prayer.

■ Have children read aloud Luke 11:1-4. Point out that Jesus used this prayer to teach *us* how to pray. Compare this prayer to a letter and its parts: the greeting, the body, and the closing. Invite children to write prayer-letters to God. Begin by greeting God, then lay needs before him. Next, thank God and then close in Jesus' name. Explain that God knows what's in their letters even as they're being written. Have children keep the letters in their Bibles to see how, when, and in what ways God answers their prayers.

38. Rainbow Promise-Streamers

Fluttery streamers remind kids that God's promises aren't a lot of air!

Point to Make: God keeps his promises.

Verse to View: I will remember my covenant.   Genesis 9:15

Preparation: You'll need plastic pop-can rings (from six-packs of soda), scissors, tape, string, and a photocopy of Take-It-Away Card 38 for each child. You'll also need these colors of crepe paper, tissue paper, or ribbon: red, orange, yellow, blue, green, and purple.

Cut tissue paper, crepe paper, or ribbon into 18-inch streamers. Cut two of every color for each child (plus one extra). Cut the plastic pop-can loops into connected pairs.

The Message

Hold up the extra streamer and say: **You know, many promises are a lot like this paper streamer. They may be colorful and bright and full of happiness. But if they're broken,** (tear the streamer in half) they can't be put back together again. Pass the streamer halves and have each child tear off a piece as he or she tells how broken promises feel. Then ask:

● **What happens if someone breaks promises over and over?**

● **Can we trust God's promises? Why?**

Say: **God knows that promises reveal a lot about us. If we're trustworthy, honest, and faithful, we don't break promises. And because God is all those things and much more, his promises are always kept! Remember when God put a rainbow in the sky as a promise to Noah and to us? What did that promise mean?** Have children tell their ideas, then say: **God promised never to destroy the world with water again—and God keeps his promises.** Read aloud Genesis 9:15, then say: **Let's make Rainbow Promise-Streamers to remind us that God always keeps his promises.**

The Meaning

Have children tape or knot two of each color streamer to the plastic loops on their pop-can rings. Then let children tie string on opposite sides of the loops to make a handle. As children work, ask questions such as "What are some things God promises us?" "How do God's promises show his love for us?" and "How can we thank God for keeping his promises?"

When the streamers are complete, wave them around. Say: **What beautiful Rainbow Promise-Streamers you've made—and how beautiful are the promises God keeps for us. Hang your streamers on a patio, in a window, or on your bicycles to remind you that God always keeps his promises. Let's close with a special Take-It-Away Card you can take home along with your Rainbow Promise-Streamers.**

Take-It-Away Card

Hand Take-It-Away Card 38 to each child as you close the message time. Have one volunteer read aloud the "Point to Make" and another the "Verse to View." End by challenging children to read the card often.

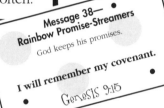

Message 38—
Rainbow Promise-Streamers

God keeps his promises.

I will remember my covenant.

Genesis 9:15

Choose-n-Use Options

● Ask children who God's best promise was, then tell them it was Jesus! Point out that God promised the world a savior and he kept that promise by giving us his Son, Jesus. Teach kids the following rhythm-rhyme. Let kids wave their Rainbow Promise-Streamers to the rhyme and clap at the appropriate time:

P-R-O-M-I-S-E

God made a promise to you and me.

He sent us Jesus from heaven above—

Clap-clap! Hooray! God's promise of love!

● Cut seven colorful paper streamers and write one letter from the word "promise" at the top of each streamer. Challenge children to think of things God promises that begin with the same letters on the streamers—for example, peace, patience, or protection for P or rejoicing or rest for R. Write the words on the streamers, then tape them around the edge of a paper plate and suspend it from a doorway for others to read and enjoy.

39. Sweet Sharing

Cute candy jars remind children to share with others.

Point to Make: God wants us to share our blessings.

Verse to View: God loves a cheerful giver. 2 Corinthians 9:7

Preparation: You'll need a Bible, baby food jars and lids, Tacky craft glue, ribbon, scissors, plastic sandwich bags, a bag of small multi-colored candies, and a photocopy of Take-It-Away Card 39 for each child.

Cut an 8-inch piece of ribbon for each child. Prepare a sandwich bag containing five of each color candy for each child.

The Message

Hand each child a sandwich bag containing candies. Say: **These are bags of pretend blessings. When I say "go," hand your blessings to each other one at a time and try to give all of them away before I say "stop." Ready? Go!** Allow one minute for children to hand their candies quickly back and forth, then say, "Stop." Ask:

▲ **What happened when you tried to give away your blessings?**

▲ **How was this game a good example of sharing with and giving to others?**

Say: **Sharing the good things we receive from God is a lot like sharing the candies in this game. The more blessings we share, the more we receive! Listen to what the Bible says about sharing good things with others.** Read aloud 2 Corinthians 9:7, 11. Then ask:

▲ **Why does God want us to give cheerfully to others?**

▲ **How does giving bring us closer to God? to others?**

Say: **God gives each of us so many good things, and we can share those good things with others who need them. What are things we can give to others?** Encourage children to tell their ideas. Then say: **Let's make some Sweet-Sharing Candy Jars to remind us how important it is to share our blessings with others.**

The Meaning

Hand each child a ribbon and a baby food jar and lid. Instruct children to remove the lids from the jars, then stack and glue the candies from their sandwich bags to the tops of the jar lids. While the lids dry, help children tie bows around the necks of the jars, then use fresh candies to partially fill their candy jars. Carefully replace the lids, but warn children that the candies may slide until the glue dries. As you work, discuss the kinds of blessings you can share with others, such as your time, talents, money, food, and other items someone may need.

Say: **Your candy jars contain candies that remind us of the sweetness of God's blessings. And to remind us about sharing those blessings, be sure to offer others a candy from your jar. See if you can give all your candy away without eating one piece for yourself!**

Let's close with a special Take-It-Away Card you can take home along with your Sweet-Sharing Candy Jar.

Take-It-Away Card

Hand Take-It-Away Card 39 to each child as you close the message time. Have one volunteer read aloud the "Point to Make" and another the "Verse to View." End by challenging children to read the card often.

Message 39—Sweet Sharing
God wants us to share our blessings.

God loves a cheerful giver.
2 Corinthians 9:7

Choose-n-Use Options

▲ As a quick community service project, let children assemble "Small-Blessings Bags." Have children fill sandwich bags with special treats such as candies, pencils, erasers, dried fruits, coupons for cookies or donuts, or other small "blessings." Tie the bags with ribbons and place a "Jesus loves you" sticker on each bag. Donate your offering to a food pantry, children's hospital, or elderly care center.

▲ Have older children read how Esau lost his birthright (his special rights of inheritance) to his brother Jacob (Genesis 25:27-34). Talk about how a birthright was like a blessing, how Esau didn't think the birthright was good enough to hold on to, and how thankful we are for each of God's blessings—no matter how large or small. End with a prayer thanking God for his blessings and asking him to show us ways to share our blessings by giving to others.

40. No Trap in a Snap

Clever Scripture holders encourage kids to learn God's precious Word.

Point to Make: We love God's Word!

Verse to View: See how I love your precepts.   Psalm 119:159

Preparation: You'll need a Bible, red construction paper, scissors, self-adhesive magnets, Tacky craft glue, markers, and a photocopy of Take-It-Away Card 40 for each child. You'll also need a new spring-type mousetrap for each child.

Cut a 2-inch red construction-paper heart for each child. Use a pair of pliers to remove the short bar that holds the spring trap from each mousetrap.

The Message

Hold up a mousetrap and ask:

■ **What's a trap?**
■ **What happens if something or someone is caught in a trap?**
■ **What "traps" do we as Christians face every day?**

Encourage children to name traps such as bad friends, dishonesty, cheating, gossiping, treating others unkindly, and saying bad words. Then ask:

■ **Why does God want us to steer clear of these traps?**
■ **What are ways we can keep out of these traps?**
■ **How can knowing what the Bible says protect us from harmful things?**

Say: **One of the best ways to steer clear of traps that hurt us is to read and know God's Word. God's Word tells us just what we need to know to stay safe and close to God! Listen to what the Bible tells us about God's Word.** Read aloud Psalm 119:159, 167. Then say: **It isn't enough to "kind of know" what God says—we need to really know, and the only way to do that is to work at learning God's Word. Let's make cool Scripture holders to hold your Take-It-Away cards and help you learn God's Word.**

The Meaning

Give each child a mousetrap, a paper heart, and a self-adhesive magnet. Let children write the words "Learn God's Word!" on their paper hearts, then glue the hearts in place on the mousetraps. Have children color the mousetraps or draw designs around the edges. Then stick a magnet on the center back of the mousetrap. Hold up a Take-It-Away Card and demonstrate how to clip the card in the spring of the trap. Encourage children to hang the Scripture-holders on their refrigerator doors and attach a new Take-It-Away Card each week. Then tell children to challenge their family members to learn the verse on the card during the week.

Say: **When we know God's Word, we can avoid getting caught in awful traps! See if you can learn the verse on today's Take-It-Away Card, then help your family learn God's Word!**

Take-It-Away Card

Hand Take-It-Away Card 40 to each child as you close the message time. Have one volunteer read aloud the "Point to Make" and another the "Verse to View." End by challenging children to read the card often.

Choose-n-Use Options

> Message 40—No Trap in a Snap
> We love God's Word! ◆
>
> ■ See how I love your precepts.
> Psalm 119:159 ■

■ Younger kids love a crazy game of Mousetrap Tag. Use a plastic laundry basket as the "mousetrap" and choose one player to be It. Have It hop after the crawling "mice" and gently trap one under the basket. The trapped mouse can say "God's Word sets me free!" and that mouse becomes the next It to carry the basket. (Older kids can repeat a verse.) End the game by offering nibbles of cheese to all the "little mice." Remind kids that not knowing God's Word is like being in a trap—and that knowing God's Word keeps us close to God.

■ Invite older children to read about the time Jesus was tempted in the desert and spoke God's Word to avoid Satan's traps (Matthew 4:1-11). Let your class choose one verse they'd like to work on learning over the next month. Explain that learning God's Word takes time, patience, and lots of dedicated love—but nothing is more worth it!

41. Harvest Helpers

Adorable pumpkin puppets teach about being Christ's helpers.

Point to Make: We're Christ's helpers.

Verse to View: The harvest is plentiful, but the workers are few.
Luke 10:2

Preparation: You'll need a Bible; green felt; green chenille wires; black and green markers; small rubber bands; fiberfill; scissors; a pair of cinnamon-color pantyhose or orange tights; and a long, sturdy twig for each child. You'll also need a photocopy of Take-It-Away Card 41 for each child.

Cut one 4-inch piece of the leg portion of a pair of pantyhose or tights for each child. The stretchy hosiery "tube" should be open on both ends. Cut one 2-inch felt leaf for each child.

The Message

Scatter the twigs on the floor and invite children to come forward and each "harvest" a twig. Ask:

● **What does it mean to "harvest" something?**
● **What kinds of things do we harvest?**
● **What might happen if crops aren't harvested?**
● **In what way is gathering crops similar to gathering people for Jesus?**

Set the twigs aside and say: **At harvest time, workers go into the fields to gather crops such as pumpkins or apples. If crops aren't harvested, fields spoil. Jesus knew the world was a lot like a big field—full of people who needed to be gathered for God. Jesus told his followers to go as workers to the harvest. Let's read what Jesus said.**
Read aloud Luke 10:2, then ask: **What do you think Jesus meant?**

Say: **Jesus didn't mean for people to pick crops, but he did mean for people to be his helpers in telling others about God's love. Let's make Harvest-Helper Puppets to learn more about being Jesus' helpers in his special harvest.**

The Meaning

Explain that you'll be making stuffed pumpkin puppets-on-a-stick. Have each child use a rubber band to attach one end of a hose piece to one end of a twig. Stuff the hosiery with fiberfill until it's plump and nearly full. Close the top of the "pumpkin" with another rubber band. (If the pumpkin flops over, slide it farther down the twig.) Slip one end of a felt leaf into the rubber band at the top of the pumpkin. Curl a chenille wire around your little finger, then twist the "tendril" around the pumpkin top. Finally, draw cute faces on the puppets. Then ask children to have their puppets tell one way to be a worker for Jesus.

Say: **It's great that we can be workers in the special field of harvest by telling others about God's love and also about Jesus' love! Now let's close with a special Take-It-Away Card you can take home along with your Harvest-Helper Puppet.**

Take-It-Away Card

Hand Take-It-Away Card 41 to each child as you close the message time. Have one volunteer read aloud the "Point to Make" and another the "Verse to View." End by challenging children to read the card often.

> **Message 41—Harvest Helpers**
>
> We're Christ's helpers.
>
> **The harvest is plentiful, but the workers are few.**
>
> Luke 10:2

Choose-n-Use Options

● Celebrate being harvest helpers by preparing "Harvest Happy-Sacks." Let children decorate small paper sacks, then fill them with a variety of fruits and nuts. Make photocopies of the following note, then staple them to the sacks. Distribute the sacks to a food pantry or to the church congregation.

Jesus said, "The harvest is plentiful, but the workers are few"—

Be a harvest helper—Jesus wants YOU!

● Challenge older children with some math fun. Read aloud Luke 10:1, 2 and point out that Jesus sent seventy-two workers into the "field." If each worker told two people about God's love, how many would be in the harvest? What if each worker told ten people? Now figure how many would be in your harvest if everyone in the class told three others about Jesus' love. Challenge kids to each tell three people about Jesus during the coming week.

42. Thank You, God

Tom Turkeys help children give thanks for God's blessings.

Point to Make: We're thankful for God's blessings.

Verse to View: Give thanks to the Lord, for he is good.   Psalm 136:1

Preparation: You'll need a Bible, paper cups, craft feathers, tape, red and yellow construction paper, markers, a bag of peanuts in the shell, and a photocopy of Take-It-Away Card 42 for each child.

No prior preparation required.

The Message

Gather children and ask:
▲ **What's the best gift someone has ever given you? Why was it the most special gift?**
▲ **In what ways are God's blessings like our most special gifts?**
▲ **What are some of the blessings, or gifts, God has given you?**
Say: **God gives us wonderful blessings such as parents and other people to love us, warm places to live, good foods to eat, schools where we learn, and churches where we worship and pray. And just as we'd say thank-you for special gifts from other people, we want to thank God for all his blessings.**
▲ **Why is it important to say, "Thank you, God?"**
▲ **How is thanking God a way to express our love for him?**
Say: **Let's see what the Bible says about thanking God.** Read aloud Psalm 136:1. Then say: **In this season of Thanksgiving, we especially want to thank God for his love and show him our love and appreciation for all he does. Let's make thankful Tom Turkeys to remind us to thank God for his love and blessings.**

The Meaning

Have children tape several "tail feathers" to the back rim of each paper cup. Then show children how to tear paper beaks and "gobblers" and tape them to the fronts of the cups. Let children draw eyes and any other features they'd like to add. As you work, visit about the special blessings God gave biblical characters, such as baby Isaac to Abraham and Sarah and great wisdom to Solomon. When the cups are complete, have each child hold up a peanut, name one blessing God has given him or her, and drop the peanut in the cup. Then have kids hold up a second peanut and tell one way to thank God, such as through sharing blessings, prayer, or even singing a thank-you song to God.

Say: **Thanking God for his blessings is important, so we want to thank God every day. Let's thank God with a prayer right now.** Pray: **Dear God, thank you for the blessings you give us in love. We love you too. Amen.**

Hand each child a handful of peanuts to put in the cup. Say: **Share these peanuts with your family and have them each name a blessing God has given them. Then share a thank-you prayer to God for all he has given.**

Now let's close with a special Take-It-Away Card you can take home along with your thankful Tom Turkey cup.

Take-It-Away Card

Hand Take-It-Away Card 42 to each child as you close the message time. Have one volunteer read aloud the "Point to Make" and another the "Verse to View." End by challenging children to read the card often.

Message 42—Thank You, God
We're thankful for God's blessings.

Give thanks to the Lord,
for he is good.

Psalm 136:1

Choose-n-Use Options

▲ Make a "blessings banner" to hang in the church entryway. Use scraps of colorful paper to decorate a 4-foot piece of shelf paper, then use crayons or markers to write blessings God has given each child on the banner. Hang the banner in a place where everyone can enjoy it. Suspend a marker beside the banner to encourage others to add their own blessings and thanks.

▲ Show two groups of older children how to read Psalm 136 responsively and taperecord the reading. Then challenge small groups to compose their own psalms of thanksgiving. Let children record their special thanks, then present the tape to another class or to the church leaders.

43. Advent Event

Colorful door hangers remind everyone to celebrate Jesus!

Point to Make: We can prepare to celebrate Jesus' birth.

Verse to View: Prepare the way for the Lord.   Isaiah 40:3

Preparation: You'll need a Bible, sprigs of evergreen, tape, twist-tie wires, scissors, and red, pink, purple, and white crepe paper. You'll also need a photocopy of Take-It-Away Card 43 for each child.

Cut 2-foot crepe paper "streamers." Cut one red, one white, one pink, and three purple streamers for each child.

The Message

Gather children and ask:

- **What are things we prepare or get ready for?**
- **How does your family prepare for Jesus' birth—or Christmas?**

Say: **In the weeks leading up to Christmas, we prepare to celebrate Jesus' birth. This time of preparation is also a time of remembering. We remember how God promised to send us a Savior—his Son, Jesus.** Read aloud Isaiah 40:3, then say: **This time of preparing for and remembering Jesus' birth is called Advent. Advent means "arrival," and during the time of Advent we prepare for the celebration of Jesus' arrival on earth long ago. Usually, we make Advent wreaths with different color candles to signify the weeks of Advent. But today let's make beautiful Advent streamers to hang on our doors to celebrate and remember Jesus' birth.**

The Meaning

Have children tape three purple streamers together at one end. Say: **In Advent, the color purple means promise, hope, and peace—all of which are found in Jesus.** Tape a pink

(or rose) streamer to the purple ones. Say: **During Advent, the color pink or rose stands for the perfect love we find in Jesus.** Tape a white streamer to the others. Say: **The color white stands for Christ's purity. Now let's add evergreen, which stands for our "forever life" with Jesus.** Use twist-tie wires to attach two sprigs of evergreen around the tape. Then say: **Finally, a red bow reminds us that Jesus lives in our hearts all year long!** Tie the red streamer into a bow and tape or wire it to the evergreen sprigs. Say: **Your door hangers are beautiful! Hang them on your front door to remind everyone to prepare for the wonderful celebration of Jesus' birth.**

Let's close with a special Take-It-Away Card you can take home along with your Advent door hanger.

Take-It-Away Card

Hand Take-It-Away Card 43 to each child as you close the message time. Have one volunteer read aloud the "Point to Make" and another the "Verse to View." End by challenging children to read the card often.

Choose-n-Use Options

Message 43—Advent Event ◆
We can prepare to celebrate Jesus' birth.

Prepare the way for the Lord.
■
Isaiah 40:3 ◆

■ Younger children will enjoy counting the weeks until Christmas with this simple Advent craft project. Have children tear green paper leaves and glue them to the sides of paper cups. Then have each child cut out three 2-by-4-inch strips of purple paper, one pink strip, and one white strip. Add torn paper "flames" to the paper "candles." Each week during Advent, tape the appropriate color candle to the edge of the paper cup "wreath." For the first three weeks, add purple candles. On the fourth week, add the pink paper candle. Then on Christmas Eve or Christmas Day, add the white paper candle.

■ Invite older children to form small groups and discuss how we can prepare for Jesus, not just during Advent or at Christmastime but throughout the year. Encourage children to mention ways such as reading the Bible, being kind to others, and living as Jesus would live. Then read the parable of the Ten Virgins (Matthew 25:1-13) and discuss how this parable is a good example of preparing for Jesus all the time.

44. The Most Special Baby

Darling ornaments remind children of Jesus' humble birth.

Point to Make: Jesus came to love us.

Verse to View: The Word became flesh.   John 1:14

Preparation: You'll need construction paper, Tacky craft glue, fishing line, scissors, self-adhesive star stickers, three craft sticks for each child, and a photocopy of Take-It-Away Card 44 for each child.

Cut an 8-inch length of fishing line for each child.

The Message

Gather children and say: **I have a riddle for you. See if you can guess what the riddle is about.**

I'm oh, so sweet and very small.
I hardly have much hair at all.
I snooze all warm inside my crib,
And when I eat, I need my bib.
Who am I?

When children have guessed "a baby," ask:

● **What is special about babies?**

● **Where do you think the special baby of a king might sleep or be born?**

Say: **Babies born into royalty or from very special families usually have the best cribs to sleep in and the best hospitals to be born in. But the most special baby of all time was born in a stable and slept in a manger. Who was that baby?** Let children tell their ideas, then say: **That baby was Jesus! Why do you think God let Jesus be born in a stable if he was so special?** Encourage children to share their thoughts. Then say: **Let's make simple stables to remind us of Jesus' birth. Then we'll learn why Jesus was born in a stable and slept in a manger.**

The Meaning

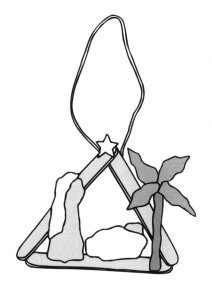

Have children glue the craft sticks into triangles. Tear out a small manger with baby Jesus tucked inside and glue it to the base of the triangle. Children may also wish to tear other figures such as Mary, Joseph, sheep, or palm trees. Glue the figures on the triangle base. Stick shiny stars at the tops of the triangles. Then tie loops of fishing line through the triangles to hang them on Christmas trees.

As children work, say: **God knew that if Jesus was born in a fancy place, people would think Jesus only came to love rich people or kings. But we know that Jesus came to love all of us. That's why Jesus was born in a small, warm stable. Jesus came to love each of us no matter who we are. Isn't that wonderful?**

Let's close with a special Take-It-Away Card to take home with your ornament. Hang the ornament on your Christmas tree to remind everyone that Jesus—the most special baby of all—came to love each of us!

Take-It-Away Card

Hand Take-It-Away Card 44 to each child as you close the message time. Have one volunteer read aloud the "Point to Make" and another the "Verse to View." End by challenging children to read the card often.

Message 44—The Most Special Baby

Jesus came to love us.

The Word became flesh.

John 1:14

Choose-n-Use Options

● Sing "Away In a Manger" as you hang your ornaments on a tree in the church entryway or at a neighboring senior care center. Add a bright star atop the tree, then share a prayer thanking God for sending Jesus to love us.

● Invite older children to read the story of Jesus' birth from Luke 2:6-14. Then have kids make simple paper costumes to help retell the story to a younger class. Make paper beards, headbands, and "animal spots." You'll need a narrator and three children to play the parts of Mary, Joseph, and the innkeeper. The rest of the children can be shepherds, angels, or animals in the stable. Invite younger children to help make animal noises. End by singing "Away in a Manger."

45. A Joyful New Noise!

New Year's noisemakers help children celebrate new lives in Jesus!

Point to Make: We can celebrate new life with Jesus.

Verse to View: Sing to the Lord a new song. *Psalm 149:1*

Preparation: You'll need a Bible, crepe paper, ribbon, scissors, tape, markers, a party hat and noisemaker, and a photocopy of Take-It-Away Card 45 for each child. You'll also need a solid-color party horn for each child.

Purchase inexpensive party horns from party shops or discount department stores. If you can't find solid-color horns, decorated ones will work.

The Message

Wear the party hat and make a lot of "joyful" noise with the noisemaker. Then say: **This is the time of year we celebrate the start of a new year. Many people like to celebrate by putting on colorful party hats, eating yummy foods, and making lots of happy noise.** Ask:

▲ **Why do you think people are so happy about the start of a new year?**

▲ **What's good about fresh, new beginnings?**

Say: **When we love Jesus and ask him to be Lord of our lives, we can have a fresh, new beginning. It's like starting a new year, only much better because we can start a new life! And that makes us want to shout with joy! Did you know that the Bible tells us to make a joyful noise? Let's see what the Bible says.** Read aloud all or part of Psalm 149. Then ask:

▲ **Why do you think people who love Jesus want to make a joyful noise?**

Say: **When we love Jesus and ask him to be Lord of our lives, we can make a joyful noise and show others how happy we are to have new life in Christ! Let's make joyous noisemakers to celebrate a new start with Jesus—and then we'll make a joyful noise!**

The Meaning

Distribute the party horns and invite children to decorate them with crepe paper streamers, ribbon, and fancy designs drawn with markers. As children work, discuss the ways we can have new life with Jesus. Point out that when we have a new life with Jesus, we follow him, pray, read the Bible, treat others kindly, and forgive others.

When the horns are finished, tell children to think about the way it feels to love Jesus, then give them five seconds to "make a joyful noise." Clap to get children's attention, then say: **Doesn't it feel good to make joyful noises? And it feels even better to love Jesus!**

Let's close with a special Take-It-Away Card you can take home along with your "make-a-joyful-noisemaker."

Take-It-Away Card

Hand Take-It-Away Card 45 to each child as you close the message time. Have one volunteer read aloud the "Point to Make" and another the "Verse to View." End by challenging children to read the card often.

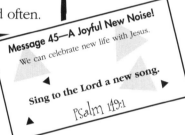

Message 45—A Joyful New Noise!
We can celebrate new life with Jesus.

◄ Sing to the Lord a new song. ►

Psalm 149:1

Choose-n-Use Options

▲ Play a variation of Duck, Duck, Goose with a game called Joyful Jog. Stand in a circle and have one child walk around the outside of the circle blowing a horn each time he or she passes another child. When the horn is blown twice beside a child, that child jogs after the one who blew the horn. The child with the horn tries to make it back to the other child's place in the circle without being tagged. Then the "chaser" becomes the next one to "make a joyful noise."

▲ Have older children explore the ways people in the New Testament celebrated Jesus. Assign small groups to read Matthew 2:1-11; 21:1-11; and 1 Corinthians 11:23-26. Compare and contrast how people long ago celebrated Jesus and how we celebrate him today. End by having each child choose one way to celebrate Jesus in the coming week.

46. I Love You Because...

Clever cutouts help children express their love for Jesus and others.

Point to Make: Jesus wants us to love others.

Verse to View: Love each other as I have loved you.   *John 15:12*

Preparation: You'll need a Bible, crayons or markers, scissors, pencils, poster board, one 8-inch square of paper for each child, and a photocopy of Take-It-Away Card 46 for each child.

Use poster board and the illustration on the facing page to make several traceable paperdoll patterns.

The Message

Gather children and say: **Let's play a little game. I'll say a sentence, then you fill in the rest. Ready? We like water because...** Encourage children to give reasons water is good. Then say: **We like going to church because...** (fill in the blank). **We love Jesus because...** (fill in the blank). Then say: **There are many reasons we like, need, or love someone or something. For example, we love Jesus because he loves us, because he died for our sins, because he forgives us, because he's making a place for us in heaven—the list goes on and on!** Ask:

- **Why is it good to recognize reasons we love Jesus?**
- **How do you think others feel when we tell them the special reasons we love them?**

Say: **Jesus told us that we can obey his commands by loving others. Let's read from the Bible.** Read aloud John 15:9-13, then ask:

- **Why does Jesus want us to love others?**

Say: **Jesus loves each of us so much—and he wants us to love others in the same way. One way we can show our love is to tell people why we love them. Let's make a special message card to give to someone we love.**

The Meaning

Hand each child a square of paper. Have children fold the paper in half, then in half again, then in a triangle. Draw the paper doll shape on the triangle, making sure the head is at the folded corners. (See illustration.) Cut out the paper dolls, being careful not to cut the folds at the hands. Have kids each think of one person they love and reasons why they love that person. Open up the paper dolls and help kids write the reasons they love their special people on the paper dolls. As children work, visit about reasons we love our families, grandparents, teachers, or friends.

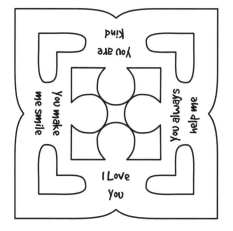

When the cards are finished, invite children to read their cards aloud. Then say: **Jesus wants us to love others, and we can tell those special people why we love them. Be sure to give your beautiful message of love to that special person!**

Now let's close with a Take-It-Away Card you can take home along with your message card.

Take-It-Away Card

Hand Take-It-Away Card 46 to each child as you close the message time. Have one volunteer read aloud the "Point to Make" and another the "Verse to View." End by challenging children to read the card often.

Choose-n-Use Options

Message 46—I Love You Because…
Jesus wants us to love others. ◆
Love each other as I have loved you.
John 15:12

■ Hide candy hearts and go on a "love safari" to find them. When all the hearts are found, have each child name a person for every candy he or she found. Then have the child tell one reason he or she loves each person. Hide the hearts and play again. Add lively music for a festive touch!

■ Form small groups and hand each group a red or white piece of poster board. Have children draw or cut out large heart shapes. Use concordances to look up references for "love" and write the entire verses on the paper hearts. Add lace and ribbons around the edges of the hearts, then hang them in a hallway where everyone will "love" looking at them!

47. Spring-Sprung!

Bouncy spring bouquets teach children that God helps us grow.

Point to Make: God helps us grow in his love.

Verse to View: Your faith is growing more and more.

2 Thessalonians 1:3

Preparation: You'll need a Bible, construction paper, scissors, long chenille wires, pencils, and a photocopy of Take-It-Away Card 47 for each child. You'll also need a plastic headband for each child.

Follow the directions in this activity to prepare a springy flower-top headband to wear. If you want longer chenille wires, simply twist two together.

The Message

Gather children and invite them to solve the following riddle. For extra fun, act out the riddle as you recite it.

I start out as a little seed—green or white or brown.
With springtime rain and lots of sun, I pop up from the ground.
What am I?

Say: **That's right—I'm a plant such as a flower or corn or grass. In other words, I'm a "growing thing."** Ask:

● **How does God help plants grow?**
● **In what ways does God help us grow?**

Say: **We're not plants, but God cares for and helps us grow just the way he tends to all his creation. God provides food and water for us—and God provides us with oodles of love! How do you think God helps us grow more in his love?** Encourage children to name ways such as through learning his Word, praying, being thoughtful to others, and loving Jesus. Then say: **Let's read what the Bible says about growing in God's love.** Read aloud 2 Thessalonians 1:3, then say: **Let's make springy springtime flowers to remind us how God helps us grow in his love.**

The Meaning

Invite children to use paper heart shapes to make two flowers. Suggest heart-shaped petals and leaves or heart shapes for the centers of the flowers. Then have each child wind two chenille wires around a pencil to make "springs." Tape paper flowers to one end of each spring, then wrap the other ends of the springs around plastic headbands to make springy "flower antennas." As children work, ask questions such as "Why does God want our love for him to grow?" and "What are ways we can encourage others to grow in God's love?"

When the flower-top headbands are complete, let children wear them and have a "flower show." Encourage each child to name one way God helps him or her grow in his love. Then say: **Thank you, God, for plants that grow—and for the love you always sow! Let's close with a special Take-It-Away Card you can take home along with your springy flower-top headband.**

Take-It-Away Card

Hand Take-It-Away Card 47 to each child as you close the message time. Have one volunteer read aloud the "Point to Make" and another the "Verse to View." End by challenging children to read the card often.

> **Message 47—Spring-Sprung!**
> God helps us grow in his love.
> **Your faith is growing more and more.**
> 2 Thessalonians 1:3

Choose-n-Use Options

● Play a lively outdoor game called Scatter, Seeds! Choose one child to be the gardener and to hold a playground ball. Have the rest of the children be the seeds and stand around the gardener. When the ball is thrown high in the air, the gardener shouts, "Scatter, seeds!" and the seeds run. When the ball is caught, the gardener shouts, "Stop, seeds!" and the seeds freeze in place. The gardener may take up to five giant steps to tag a seed with the ball. Then that seed becomes the next gardener.

● Let older children write verses about God's love on a 12-foot length of cash register or adding machine tape. Color the tape green, then glue one end of the tape in the bottom of a plastic margarine container. Roll the tape. Make a large construction-paper flower to glue to the end of the tape. Cut a slit in the lid large enough for the flower to slip through. When the flower is pulled, *voilà*—up grows a Scripture posy! Give your project to a church leader for a special springtime lift.

48. Easter Storytelling Eggs

Cute eggs invite children to retell the greatest love story ever!

Point to Make: Jesus is alive!

Verse to View: He has risen!   Mark 16:6

Preparation: You'll need a twig, shiny star stickers, a small piece of cloth, scissors, candy hearts, small pebbles, and a photocopy of Take-It-Away Card 48 for each child. You'll also need a plastic pull-apart egg for each child.

Cut apart the star stickers, leaving the back paper in place. If you can't find candy hearts, use heart stickers.

The Message

Gather children and ask:

▲ **What's your favorite story? Why is it your favorite?**
▲ **Do you know what the happiest story in the world is?**

Let children tell their ideas, then say: **The story of the first Easter is the happiest story ever—and this is a *true* story! Since it's Easter time, let's make special Easter Storytelling Eggs. Then you can share the happiest story ever with everyone.**

The Meaning

Hand each child a plastic pull-apart egg. Tell the following story as children add the appropriate story "props" to their eggs. **Jesus came to love, heal, and teach people about God. But there were people who didn't believe Jesus was God's Son. These mean people wanted to hurt Jesus. So they hung Jesus on a wooden cross to die.** Hold up the twig and have each child snap off a small piece to place in the egg as a remembrance of the wooden cross. **Jesus died on the cross, but he died so our sins could be forgiven and we could be God's friends. Thank you, Jesus. Then Jesus' friends wrapped his body in a soft cloth.** Snip off tiny pieces of fabric to add to the eggs. **They laid Jesus in a cave-like tomb and sealed the tomb with a large stone.** Let each child choose a pebble to represent the stone. **After three days—on Easter morning—Jesus' friends came to the tomb and saw an angel brighter than stars!** Place a star sticker in each egg. **"Jesus is alive!" said the angel. So the friends ran to tell everyone that Jesus is alive—and that he loves us!**

Say: **Jesus was raised to life on Easter morning. Jesus overcame death so we can live forever with God. Jesus is alive! What a story of joy and love!**

▲ **Why do you think this is the happiest story ever told?**

▲ **Why do you think it's important for people to hear this wonderful story?**

▲ **Who can you tell this happy story to today? this week?**

Say: **You can tell others the good news about how Jesus is alive by using your special Easter Storytelling Eggs. Let's close with a special Take-It-Away Card you can take home along with your pretty egg.** (If you have extra time, invite children to decorate the eggs with stickers and permanent markers.)

Take-It-Away Card

Hand Take-It-Away Card 48 to each child as you close the message time. Have one volunteer read aloud the "Point to Make" and another the "Verse to View." End by challenging children to read the card often.

Message 48—Easter Storytelling Eggs

Jesus is alive! ▶

He has risen! ▶

▲ Mark 16:6

Choose-n-Use Options

▲ Invite children to make darling eggs with a message by decorating plastic pull-apart eggs with markers and stickers. Make a photocopy of the following rhyme to slip inside each egg along with a marshmallow bunny. Present the eggs to a senior care center or children's home.

This bunny's hopping up to say, "Jesus is alive today!"

He has risen. Mark 16:6

49. Parents Color the World

Whimsical pins help kids express their special love on Mother's Day and Father's Day.

Point to Make: God gave us parents and other caring adults to love.

Verse to View: Children, obey your parents in everything.
Colossians 3:20

Preparation: You'll need a Bible, small colorful beads, red felt, scissors, two large diaper pins or safety pins for each child, and a photocopy of Take-It-Away Card 49 for each child.

Purchase small beads such as "seed beads" or "pony beads" from most craft stores. Cut two 3-inch felt heart shapes for each child. Arrange for a time children can present their special gifts to their parents or to other special persons in their lives.

The Message

Gather children and say: **God has given us so many wonderful gifts, and one of the most loving of those gifts is our parents or other loving adults. What are some of the things your parents or other loving adults do for you?** Encourage children to tell their ideas, then ask:

■ **In what ways did God express his love by giving us parents?**

■ **How can we express love to our parents or other loving caregivers?**

Say: **The Bible tells us one way to express our love is through obeying our parents.** Read aloud Colossians 3:20, then say: **Other ways to express our love include telling our parents how special they are. Let's make colorful pins for our parents or other loved ones to wear. The pins will remind us all how glad we are that God gave us parents and special adults to love!**

The Meaning

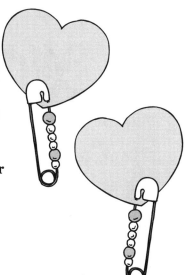

Hand each child two diaper pins. Say: **These big pins remind us of how sweetly our parents cared for us when we were babies. We'll put different colored beads on each of the pins. Think of one thing about your mom or dad that each color reminds you of. For example, yellow might be for the sunshine your dad brings to your life or blue could be for the way your mom chases away your "blues" or green might be for your mom's favorite color. Make one pin for your mom and one for your dad—or pins to give other adults you love.** Encourage children to tell each other what each color represents.

When the pins are complete, hand each child two felt hearts. Have children pin the tips of the beaded pins to the bottoms of the hearts. Then invite children to present their gifts of love to their parents or other special adults. Be sure to have children tell the recipients what each color bead represents. End the presentation time with big hugs. Then say: **Let's close with a special Take-It-Away Card you can take home.**

Take-It-Away Card

Hand Take-It-Away Card 49 to each child as you close the message time. Have one volunteer read aloud the "Point to Make" and another the "Verse to View." End by challenging children to read the card often.

Choose-n-Use Options

Message 49—Parents Color the World
◆ God gave us parents and other caring adults to love.

Children, obey your parents in everything.

■ Colossians 3:20 ◆

- Invite parents to a simple—but simply great—party. Decorate balloons with heart shapes, then frost and decorate prepared sugar cookies. Encourage children to introduce their parents or special loved ones and tell one special thing about them, such as "My dad makes the best pizza in the world!" or "My grandma bowls better than I do!"

- Have older children research "whose parent is whom?" Let small groups find out who was Jesus' mom (Luke 2:5-7), who was Isaac's dad (Genesis 21:3), who was Samuel's mom (1 Samuel 1:20), and who was Solomon's dad (2 Chronicles 1:1). Invite groups to report their findings to the entire class. Point out the importance parents played throughout the Bible and how important, needed, and loved they are today.

50. Christian Fireworks

Festive pretend fireworks help children understand what being a Christian means.

Point to Make: Christians are loyal to Jesus.

Verse to View: It is the Lord Christ you are serving. *Colossians 3:24*

Preparation: You'll need a Bible, plastic drinking straws, tape, and a photocopy of Take-It-Away Card 50 for each child. You'll also need red, purple, gold, and green shredded polyester film.

Shiny shredded polyester film is used to fill gift bags. Purchase bags of shredded polyester film at most craft or party supply stores.

The Message

This message works well for any national holiday—or any time you want to present a message on "loyalty." Gather children and say: **I have a rhyme for you. See if you can guess what I am.**

I shoot up in the nighttime sky—whoosh—above our nation.
I explode in many colors bright—what a celebration!
What am I?

When children have guessed that you are "fireworks," say: **Fireworks are beautiful and used to celebrate many holidays—especially holidays celebrating loyalty to our country.** Ask:

● **What does it mean if we're loyal to someone or something?**
● **Can we be loyal to God? to Jesus?**
● **What are ways to show our loyalty to Jesus?**
● **Why do you think Jesus wants us to be loyal to him?**

Say: **Christians love Jesus and want to be loyal to him. That means we stand behind Jesus and believe in all he teaches us. Being a loyal Christian means living the way Jesus wants us to live. Let's see what the Bible says about being loyal to Christ.**
Read aloud Colossians 3:24, then say: **We can make beautiful pretend fireworks to celebrate being Christians who are loyal to Jesus.**

The Meaning

Hand each child a drinking straw and set out the different colors of polyester film and tape. Have each child tape two purple polyester film streamers to one end of their straws as you say: **The color purple in our fireworks stands for Jesus' royalty as God's Son. Because of Jesus' royalty, we want to show our loyalty!** Tape on two red streamers and say: **Red stands for our hearts and our loyal love for Jesus.** Add two gold streamers and say: **Shiny gold reminds us of the treasure we have in Jesus—and how loyal Christians are worth so much more than gold!** Add two green streamers and say: **Green is for the everlasting life we can have through Jesus. Now wave your "fireworks-on-a-stick" and let's be joyful that we're loyal Christians who know, love, and follow Jesus! Hooray!**

After several waves of your sparkly make-believe fireworks, say: **Let's close with a special Take-It-Away Card you can take home along with your Christian fireworks.**

Take-It-Away Card

Hand Take-It-Away Card 50 to each child as you close the message time. Have one volunteer read aloud the "Point to Make" and another the "Verse to View." End by challenging children to read the card often.

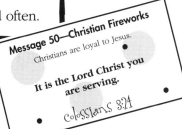

Message 50—Christian Fireworks

Christians are loyal to Jesus.

It is the Lord Christ you are serving.

Colossians 3:24

Choose-n-Use Options

● Your kids will love making another crafty "fireworks display" to celebrate their joy in Jesus. Put drops of red, yellow, and blue tempera paint onto white paper, then invite children to blow on the paint through drinking straws. The colors will squiggle and run into an explosion of color! Display the artwork on a door with the caption: "Celebrate Jesus!" For extra fun, add crepe paper around the display and tape several balloons to the door.

● Write the word "loyalty" in a column on poster board, then have children brainstorm words that describe Christian traits beginning with each letter. For example, L might stand for "love" and O for "obedient." When your list of words is complete, discuss ways a Christian develops each of those traits.

Scripture Verses for Mezuzah Tubes

I delight in your decrees; I will not neglect your word.

Psalm 119:16

Your word is a lamp to my feet and a light for my path.

Psalm 119:105

All Scripture is God-breathed and is useful for teaching, rebuking, correcting, and training in righteousness.

2 Timothy 3:16

Fix these words of mine in your hearts and minds.

Deuteronomy 11:18

How sweet are your words to my taste, sweeter than honey to my mouth!

Psalm 119:103

All your words are true; all your righteous laws are eternal.

Psalm 119:160

Wing Pattern for the Bee-Attitudes

Be humble.
Be comforted.
Be meek.
Be fair and just.

Be merciful.
Be pure in heart.
Be peacemakers.
Be faithful.

Message 1—Prayer Bears

Jesus wants us to pray for others.

I pray for them.

John 17:9

Message 2—The Inside Story

God looks at our hearts—not our outward appearances.

The Lord looks at the heart.

1 Samuel 16:7

Message 3—Love That Light!

We can shine our love to others.

You are the light of the world.

Matthew 5:14

Message 4—Wave Your Choice

We choose to serve God.

But as for me and my household, we will serve the Lord.

Joshua 24:15

Message 5—Temper Tornadoes

Prayer calms our anger.

Get rid of all bitterness, rage and anger.

Ephesians 4:31

Message 6—Hip-Hop!

When we tell God we'll do something, we hop to it!

Jonah obeyed the word of the Lord and went to Nineveh.

Jonah 3:3

Message 7—Mezuzah Tubes

God's Word is important to learn and remember.

I will not neglect your word.

Psalm 119:16

Message 8—Hide It in Your Heart

God's Word is alive in our hearts.

I have hidden your word in my heart.

Psalm 119:11

Message 9—Teacher, Teach Me

God wants us to be teachable.

I am the Lord your God, who teaches you what is best for you.

Isaiah 48:17

Message 10—The Golden Ruler

We treat others as we want to be treated.

Do to others what you would have them do to you.

Matthew 7:12

Message 11—Kindness Confetti

God wants us to speak kindly.

Therefore encourage one another.

I Thessalonians 5:11

Message 12—All Around the World

We can pray for others around the world.

We are therefore Christ's ambassadors.

2 Corinthians 5:20

Message 13—Anything Bags

God can do anything.

Is anything too hard for the Lord?

Genesis 18:14

Message 14—No Bones About It!

God made us in a wonderful way.

I praise you because I am fearfully and wonderfully made.

Psalm 139:14

Message 15—Save to Give

God wants us to give to others.

It is more blessed to give than to receive.

Acts 20:35

Message 16—Creation Celebration

We're thankful for God's creation.

God saw all that he had made, and it was very good.

Genesis 1:31

Message 17—Worship Bells

We worship God for who he is and for what he does.

Come, let us bow down in worship.

Psalm 95:6

Message 18—Mission of Love

We're Christ's missionaries.

How beautiful are the feet of those who bring good news!

Romans 10:15

Message 19—Bee-Attitudes

We can live as Jesus wants us to live.

If we live, we live to the Lord.

Romans 14:8

Message 20—Follow-Me Friends

God is with us all the time.

The Lord your God will be with you wherever you go.

Joshua 1:9

Message 21—Our Giving God

God gives us what we need.

My God will meet all your needs.

Philippians 4:19

Message 22—Hooray for Help

We can help each other.

Be kind and compassionate to one another.

Ephesians 4:32

Message 23—20/20 Vision

God sees everything.

The Lord looks down and sees all mankind.

Psalm 33:13

Message 24—A "Fishy" Hello

Christians stick together.

I thank my God every time I remember you.

Philippians 1:3

Message 25—Believe-It Balloons

Faith is believing what we can't always see.

Now faith is being sure of what we hope for and certain of what we do not see.

Hebrews 11:1

Message 26—Team Jesus

We're all winners with Jesus.

He [God] gives us the victory through our Lord Jesus Christ.

1 Corinthians 15:57

Message 27—Symbol of Love

Jesus died for us.

And he died for all.

2 Corinthians 5:15

Message 28—Who Is the Holy Spirit?

The Holy Spirit helps us.

The Holy Spirit, whom the Father will send in my name, will teach you all things.

John 14:26

Message 29—Near to God

We can be closer to God.

Come near to God and he will come near to you.

James 4:8

Message 30—God's Armor

We can put on God's protection every day.

Put on the full armor of God.

Ephesians 6:11

Message 31—Wobbly Walkers

Jesus is the only path to God.

No one comes to the Father except through me.

John 14:6

Message 32—Meet-n-Treat

Treat others as you would treat Jesus.

Whatever you did for one of the least of these brothers of mine, you did for me.

Matthew 25:40

Message 33—Our Special Names

Jesus knows our names.

He calls his own sheep by name.

John 10:3

Message 34—Focus of Faith

We want our focus to be on Jesus.

Let us fix our eyes on Jesus.

Hebrews 12:2

Message 35—Step by Step

Trusting Jesus comes step by step.

Trust in God; trust also in me.

John 14:1

Message 36—Mold Me, God

God molds us as he desires.

We are the clay, you are the potter.

Isaiah 64:8

Message 37—Prayer Fingers

There is God's power in prayer.

The prayer of a righteous man is powerful and effective.

James 5:16

Message 38— Rainbow Promise-Streamers

God keeps his promises.

I will remember my covenant.

Genesis 9:15

Message 39—Sweet Sharing

God wants us to share our blessings.

God loves a cheerful giver.

2 Corinthians 9:7

Message 40—No Trap in a Snap

We love God's Word!

See how I love your precepts.

Psalm 119:159

Message 41—Harvest Helpers

We're Christ's helpers.

The harvest is plentiful, but the workers are few.

Luke 10:2

Message 42—Thank You, God

We're thankful for God's blessings.

Give thanks to the Lord, for he is good.

Psalm 136:1

Message 43—Advent Event ◆

We can prepare to celebrate Jesus' birth.

Prepare the way for the Lord.

Isaiah 40:3

Message 44—The Most Special Baby

Jesus came to love us.

The Word became flesh.

John 1:14

Message 45—A Joyful New Noise!

We can celebrate new life with Jesus.

Sing to the Lord a new song.

Psalm 149:1

Message 46—I Love You Because . . .

Jesus wants us to love others. ◆

Love each other as I have loved you.

John 15:12

Message 47—Spring-Sprung!

God helps us grow in his love.

Your faith is growing more and more.

2 Thessalonians 1:3

Message 48—Easter Storytelling Eggs

Jesus is alive!

He has risen!

Mark 16:6

Message 49—Parents Color the World

God gave us parents and other caring adults to love.

Children, obey your parents in everything.

Colossians 3:20

Message 50—Christian Fireworks

Christians are loyal to Jesus.

It is the Lord Christ you are serving.

Colossians 3:24

Index